# TwinInsanity

## PART 7

J Ware

ISBN-13: 978-1-950650-56-9

# Prologue

It was the day after everyone found out that Jovanni was in a coma. Nathan had been speaking to the doctor, in regards to Jovanni's condition, so he could relay it in layman's terms, to his brother. Maxwell had no way to get in touch with Ricky, so Michael took care of it; he looked up Randall Hepner and then got in contact with him, so he could relay the message. Maxwell had to leave, to check on the twins. Malcolm was still at Bernadine's house and taking care of them; he stayed at her house, so Maxwell could return to the hospital. Cyrus and Nathan had also returned to the hospital.

*    *    *

In Houston, Lydia walked to the door and then opened it; before she could get a word out, she was punched in the face. Lydia yelled, as she fell back and on to the floor. Ricky walked in and had Shooter and Bullet with him. Bullet closed the door, after the guys walked in.

Lydia looked up at Ricky with her hand to her face. "Get out of here!" Ricky shook his head, and then bent down to grab Lydia by the hair; he rose back up and pulled her up with him. She winced in pain, as he held her hair tight, and then jerked her head towards him. She was crying now and terrified.

Ricky slightly leaned his head to the side, as he stared at her. "Where Jaquelyn at?" Lydia sniffed and then winced, as he tightened his grip on her hair. "I…I don't know." Ricky shook his head. "Wrong answer, bitch…" Ricky let Lydia's hair go, and then backhanded her across the face. Lydia flung around, and back down to the floor again; she cried hard, as he yelled for her to shut up.

Lydia looked back up at Ricky, and then shook her head. "I don't know where Jaquelyn is…why would I know?" Ricky stepped closer to Lydia, and she slightly flinched, when she thought, he was going to hit her again. He knelt down to her level, with an angry look on his face. "JoJo's in the hospital in Dallas…Jaquelyn stabbed her yesterday, and now JoJo's in a coma. Jaquelyn's on the run, and I know if she'd go to anybody, then it'd be you first. So, where she at?" Lydia slightly shook her head. "I swear, I don't know…I didn't know she did that. I don't talk to Jaquelyn anymore." Ricky looked at Bullet and Shooter. "Tear this bitch up…" Bullet nodded, and then he and Shooter walked away, to go through bedrooms and every inch of the house, while searching for anything or anyone.

Lydia watched the guys walk away, and then looked back at Ricky. "Ricky, please…they don't have to do that; she's not here and I don't know where she's at. Please don't hurt me anymore." Ricky grabbed Lydia again and then pulled her up from the floor, by her hair again. She continued to be in pain and cry, as he kept his grip on her. "You know me, Bellfort Randy…you know what happens to muthafuckas that lie to me. If you lyin' to me, then I'ma come back and fuck you up…or maybe just kill you, 'cause you really useless to me…always was." Lydia swallowed hard, as she stared at him. She slightly nodded her head. "I understand…but she's not here, and she wouldn't come to me anyway, if something like that happened."

Ricky walked with Lydia and then to the living room; he flung her on the couch, and she looked at him. He stood there, and then looked at his watch, before looking back at her. "If you hear from Jaquelyn…then you call me. If I hear you in touch with her and you didn't tell me, then I'ma come back for you." She stared at Ricky while terrified and couldn't speak.

Shortly after, Bullet and Shooter walked into the living room and Ricky looked at them. "Y'all find something?" The guys shook their heads, and then Shooter spoke. "Nothing here…the bedrooms clear and nothing in the master that say Jaquelyn was here." Ricky nodded and then looked back at Lydia. "You heard what I said…I'ma be back." Ricky looked at the guys then jerked his head. They all walked out the living room, and then left the house. Lydia put her hand to her mouth and cried loudly, while in much pain. Knowing what Jaquelyn did and what could happen to her, if Jaquelyn did get in contact with her, Lydia prayed that Jaquelyn stayed away.

# Chapter 1

Two months later…

During the course of a couple of months, Jovanni's condition still hadn't changed; she was still in a coma in Dallas. Cyrus had to make arrangements to hurry and move to Dallas, to be with Bernadine and visit Jovanni in the hospital; he found work and got a transfer from the job he was at in Houston, to another branch in Dallas. Nathan helped his brother move and was saddened to see him go but understood that he was a husband now and had to be with his wife. Maxwell had his twins in Dallas with him; he was taking care of them while Jovanni was in the hospital. Ricky and Shooter were still in Houston and looking for Jaquelyn, who was still missing; a warrant was out for her arrest. Bernadine was in her sixth month of her pregnancy and was taking it easy, as her doctor told her to. Cyrus did as he said and took care of her, while not letting her lift a finger to do anything. At this point, and with her complications with her high blood pressure, Bernadine was bedridden.

*     *     *

In Houston, Lydia was about to leave her home, when the doorbell rang; she walked the rest of the way to the front, and then opened the door. Lydia frowned and then tried to slam the door shut, but it was stopped, by Jaquelyn's hand.

Jaquelyn pushed her way in and then closed the door behind her; she locked it and then took her shades off, as Lydia shook her head. "No, get out of here…leave now." Jaquelyn frowned, as she stared at her mama. "Really? So, now you're turning your back on me too?" Lydia frowned. "Turn my back on you? You stopped talking to me, first. That doesn't matter anyway, and I don't care…you need to leave and never come back here."

Jaquelyn stepped closer to her mama, and Lydia stepped back from her. "Don't, Jaquelyn…I know what you did to your sister; she's still in a coma." Jaquelyn frowned. "A coma? I just stabbed her, but it was an accident…I was defending myself; she attacked me first and…" Lydia interjected. "I don't wanna hear anymore, so just stop…I don't know anything, and I didn't hear anything, so get out of here." Jaquelyn shook her head. "Why won't you help me? I can't go back home, and I can't trust anyone…I don't have anyone else." Lydia shook her head no. "I'm not dying for you…I know you're unstable, but if Ricky finds out you were here, then he'll kill me. He's probably watching the house right now, so leave me alone and turn yourself in." Jaquelyn frowned. "You won't die for me, huh? I guess I'm not worth it either, to you." Lydia rolled her eyes. "You stabbed your sister…you're on the run now and a wanted woman; there's nothing I can do to help you. The police have already been here, and I'd rather have them come back, then Ricky."

Jaquelyn stared at her mama, and then shook her head while in disgust. "JoJo stabbed a man and killed him, in self-defense, like she said…just like I did. You called Ricky to help her, so why not me…? Why not me, mama?" Lydia swallowed hard, and then her eyes became watery. "Jaquelyn…I'd understand more if you stabbed Lionel and killed him, but not JoJo. She has a lot more people that have her back than you do and ever will, so turn yourself in or go back to wherever you've been for the past two months." Jaquelyn shook her head. "I can't…I can't go back to Preston, because he'll possibly kill me if he finds out he's harboring a fugitive; he won't want anything to do with me either." Lydia shook her head. "Then where will you go?" Jaquelyn slightly shrugged her shoulders. "Give me the keys to the lake house in Dallas." Lydia slightly nodded her head. "They're hanging on the wall…"

Jaquelyn walked to the wall, where the keys were hanging, and then recognized the keys she was looking for. She grabbed the lake house keys, as Lydia spoke. "Leave, Jaquelyn…and don't ever come back." Jaquelyn turned to look at her mama, after she grabbed the keys; she swallowed hard, and then wiped her eyes. Jaquelyn slightly nodded her head, and then put her shades back on, before turning around and walking out the house. Lydia watched her leave and then put her hand to her mouth; she cried hard, as she walked to the living room. She hated to turn her daughter away, but Lydia didn't want to lose her life, as she knew she would.

Lydia grabbed her cellphone and then dialed a number; she waited while the phone rang on the other end. Someone answered. "Uh, Ricky…it's Lydia; she was just here…she left with keys to a lake house, I have in Dallas. I'll text you the address."

# Chapter 2

In Dallas, Maxwell had just returned from court, and then entered the law firm; he greeted others on the way in, and then stopped at the receptionist's desk to grab his mail. He went through his mail, as he walked to his office; he was stopped by Michael. Maxwell looked at his brother. "Hey…" Michael nodded, as Maxwell walked into his office; Michael followed behind, and then closed the door after he walked in. "So, what's going on, Mike?" Michael shook his head, as he walked over to Maxwell's desk. "Nothing much, I'm just worried about you. You walk around like a robot on steroids." Maxwell looked at his brother and frowned; he sat down in his chair and then made a sarcastic sound. "Well, I'm sorry that my composure is annoying you." Michael sighed and then sat down in the chair across from his brother's desk. "It's not annoying me, but since JoJo has been in the hospital, you haven't showed any type of emotion, like you did at the hospital the first night. Are you alright?"

Maxwell looked down at his mail, and then back up again at his brother. "I'm fine, Mike…I'm working and going home to my kids, who are being watched by a real nanny…Angeline…" Michael rolled his eyes, as Maxwell continued. "And I'm just great…life is great, my job is great, and my kids are great…I'm great." Michael raised an eyebrow, as he stared at his brother. "No, you're not, Max…you're holding in how you really feel and it's not good to do that. I know it's been kind of rough for you these past couple of months, but…" Maxwell interjected, as he stood from his chair. "Kind of rough? It's been more than kind of rough; it's been hell, Mike. I've already been through this before with JoJo being in a damn coma. I'm losing my mind every day…I miss my baby, and I need her to come out of this coma, alive for me and our children. I can't live without her…" Maxwell's eyes became watery, and then Michael stood from the chair.

Maxwell shook his head, as he sniffed, and then Michael walked over to him. "Max, I'm here for you…everybody is here for you. JoJo made it out of this before, so she's gonna make it out of this again." Maxwell looked at his brother, and then sniffed again. "But what if she doesn't? What do I tell our twins?" Michael sighed and then shook his head. "Don't worry about that, Max…just keep doing what you're doing and taking care of your babies; they'll see their mama again soon." Maxwell wiped his face and then nodded; it was the first time that he showed this emotion to anyone, of how he felt about Jovanni being in a coma.

Maxwell cleared his throat, and then nodded to his brother. "I'm fine now…I just had to get that out. I'm ok, Mike, so you can go back to work." Michael slightly nodded his head. "Ok, well I only have a few more hours and then I'm going home." Maxwell nodded and then Michael told his brother he would see him later. Michael turned around and walked away from his brother; he then left the office. Afterwards, Maxwell sat back down in his chair, and then put both hands over his face, to continue crying in private.

*   *   *

It was later in the evening, and Michael was home from work; he entered his house and then hung his keys on the wall. Michael walked to his office first and then put his briefcase away; he then walked out his office and headed towards the stairs. He walked up the stairs, and then went to his bedroom. Stacee thought he heard something and then walked out the boys' nursery; they were eight months old now.

Stacee walked to Michael's bedroom and then walked in, since the door was open. He heard the shower so knew that Michael was home from work and taking a shower now. The doorbell rang and continued to ring, so Stacee walked out the bedroom and then hurried downstairs, since the boys were asleep.

The doorbell rang again, and Stacee sucked his teeth, as he jogged the rest of the way to the front door. Once at the door, he opened it; he then frowned and before he could say a word, Aubrey pushed Stacee out the way to go in the house. Stacee slammed the door and then turned around, but Aubrey wasn't there.

Stacee called out for Aubrey, since he knew that was his name now.

Aubrey went to the den, and then was standing at the window. Stacee walked in the den, and then stopped. "What the fuck? Get the hell out of here, man." Aubrey looked at Stacee. "I'ma leave in a little bit, so why don't you go clean the house or something?" Stacee frowned. "Mike is home, so either you get the fuck out now, or he's gonna make you leave." Aubrey looked out the window, and then back to Stacee. "This won't take long, so go find something to do, and leave me the fuck alone." Stacee clenched his jaw. "You're really starting to piss me off, Aubrey." Aubrey frowned, and then turned all the way around to Stacee. "Don't say my damn name…the only one that can say my name is Mike…and he said it plenty of times, when we used to fuck." Stacee frowned and made his way over to Aubrey, as he spoke. "Oh, yeah? Well, keep reminiscing, because you won't ever hear it like that again." Aubrey sucked his teeth. "Please man, you don't mean shit to him…and it don't matter anyway, because I don't want him back." Stacee threw his hands up. "Then why the fuck are you here?!" Before Aubrey could speak, someone else did. "I'd like to know the same damn thing." Stacee turned around and saw Michael; Aubrey saw him too.

Michael slowly walked into the den with a towel wrapped around his waist; he looked at Stacee and then back to Aubrey. "What are you doing here?" Aubrey sighed. "I just need a place to stand for a few minutes…why? Is seeing me making you feel some type of way?" Stacee rolled his eyes, and Michael sarcastically laughed. "Uh no, Aubrey, so get the hell out of my house…you can stand outside my damn door." Aubrey walked away from the window, and then over to Michael. "How about I stand right here…Mike. You toss me to the side for this reject that don't give a fuck about you. Now you act like you don't know me. So, we can't be friends, either?" Michael rolled his eyes, as Aubrey eyed him. Stacee looked at Michael. "Why don't you let me throw him out? The reject that lives here." He looked at Aubrey, who then looked at him; Aubrey gave him a snide look. "Shut the fuck up…"

Stacee was about to go over to Aubrey, when Michael interjected. "Stacee…don't; just leave it alone, because Aubrey is apparently a lunatic." Aubrey looked back at Michael. "That's what you think of me?" Michael sighed, and then slightly squinted his eyes; he said nothing, as he walked around Aubrey and then over to the window. Aubrey turned around. "Don't do that, Mike…" Michael looked out the window, and then frowned; he then looked back at Aubrey. "Why is Kentay and Auston outside my house?" Stacee looked at Aubrey, as Aubrey sighed and then cleared his throat. "Kentay left his key card, so Auston said he'd meet him here…while I was in the car with Kentay." Michael frowned and then shook his head, as he walked away from the window. "You're a piece of work, Aubrey." Michael walked out the den, and Aubrey went after him, as he spoke. "What's that supposed to mean?" Stacee went after them.

Michael reached the living room, and then turned around to Aubrey. "So, now you're cheating with Kentay, when you know he's with Auston? Are you destined to break-up everybody's relationship?" Aubrey frowned. "It just happened…" Michael made a sarcastic sound. "Just happened, my ass…just like it just happened when you fucked Auston behind my back. I guess you're taking back what's yours now." Aubrey rolled his eyes. "Auston was never mine…we just fucked, and I said I was sorry for that. I went to Kentay after you dropped me on Christmas Eve; he made the first move, because he never stopped wanting me. So, what are you mad about, Mike? What do you care who or what I do?" Michael put his hands up, and then dropped them. "You're right, I don't care and it's none of my damn business, but you're not about to hide in my fucking house because you're too scared to face being caught cheating once again. If it's not a big deal, then take your ass out there and tell Auston that you're fucking his man."

Aubrey stared at Michael, and then turned his head to the side. Michael slowly nodded his head. "Yeah, that's what I thought…when you're done hiding, get out of my house." Michael sat down on the couch and then Stacee glanced at Aubrey, before he walked over to the bar. "You want a drink, Mike?" Michael slowly nodded his head, as he stared at Aubrey. "Yes…" Stacee made Mike a drink, as Aubrey sighed.

Before Aubrey could say another word, the doorbell rang, and Stacee walked away from the bar with Michael's drink; he handed Mike the drink and then walked past Aubrey, out the living room. Aubrey watched him and then looked back at Michael. "So, you just wanted somebody to wait on you, hand and foot?" Michael frowned, as he looked at Aubrey. "He's my damn nanny, housekeeper, and everything else rolled all into one…that's what I pay him for." Aubrey shook his head. "Right…and you're not fucking him?" Stacee walked back into the living room and had someone behind him.

# Chapter 3

Kentay stopped in the living room and looked at Michael, before looking at Aubrey. "He's not leaving, so you're gonna have to go back to Houston." Aubrey sighed and then nodded. "Yeah, alright…is he still out there?" Kentay sighed and then nodded. "Yeah, he's gonna follow me back to my place, so I don't know what you want me to do. You need to get your car from my place, before we get there. I'ma stall him and tell him I need to stop by the store, but you have to find another way over there." Aubrey put his hand over his face, and then dropped it; he hated what he was about to do next. "Uh, Mike…can you please take me to Kentay's house, so I can pick up my car, please?" Stacee frowned, and then Michael sighed.

Kentay cleared his throat. "Auston is waiting outside, so I'ma head out. Text me when you get your car, so we can head there." Aubrey looked at him and then nodded. Kentay glanced at Michael, and then turned to walk out the living room. Afterwards, Aubrey looked back at Michael. "I know I was just an ass, but come on, Mike…please?" Michael leaned forward and then set his glass on the coffee table; he then stood from the couch. "I'm not taking you anywhere…but Stacee can take you." Stacee frowned, as he shot Michael a look. "What? Are you for real?" Michael looked at him and then nodded. "I'm gonna go get ready for my date tonight…" Stacee raised an eyebrow. "Date?" Michael nodded, and then said he was going to get dressed.

Michael unwrapped his towel and then held it in his hand, as he walked out the living room, while naked. Aubrey stared hard, until Michael was out of sight. Stacee looked at him and then clenched his jaw, as Aubrey slowly shook his head. "Damn, I miss that…" Aubrey continued to shake his head, as he walked out the living room. Stacee sighed and then walked out too; he grabbed the keys on the way out the house with Aubrey.

It was close to an hour later, when Stacee returned to the house. He hung the keys on the wall and then called out for Michael, as he made his way through the house. Stacee went up the stairs and took them two at a time; he then went to Michael's bedroom, where the door was open. Michael was lying on the bed and watching television, in his underwear. Stacee walked in and then made a sarcastic sound. "I see you have underwear on now…maybe you should of had that on earlier, when Aubrey was here." Michael turned his head to Stacee, and then slightly laughed. "It's not like you or him hadn't seen it before." Stacee frowned, as he walked over to the bed. "I saw it after you pulled out of some dude…Aubrey saw it in a personal way. I guess you're giving him something to reminisce on."

Michael rolled his eyes, as Stacee spoke again. "And you should of let Aubrey get caught cheating, instead of saving his ass. He did cheat on you, so I'd think you wouldn't want that to happen to anybody else." Michael sighed, as he stared at Stacee. "Are you done scolding me, like you're my damn daddy?" Stacee shook his head, and then turned around to leave. Michael sighed. "Stacee…" He turned around at the door and looked at Michael. "I'm sorry, but Kentay is just my damn mechanic, not my friend…and Auston is not my friend either; he's supposed to be Aubrey's friend. None of that shit was my business." Stacee put his hand up and then dropped it. "You know what, it's none of my business either…so whatever. I thought you had a damn date to get ready for."

Michael sighed and then turned his head away, as Stacee frowned; he then slightly nodded his head. "I see you're playing games with your ex now." Michael looked back at him. "I'm not playing games, but he's been suspecting that me and you are fucking since day one. I know we're not, so for him to believe we're not, then I said I had a date in front of him, so he'd stop asking. Aubrey already knows how I used to do it, so I knew he'd believe that." Stacee rubbed his hands down his face and then sighed, as he stared at Michael. "I been trying to talk to you for a while, since you got that call about JoJo. I didn't think it was important anymore after that news, but maybe it's time now." Michael slightly nodded his head, and then Stacee continued. "Maybe you don't have a date tonight, but you went back to your extracurricular activities." Michael frowned, as Stacee continued. "My point is, if you wanna keep throwing these other guys in my face, then I can move back out and just come watch the boys during the day."

Michael rose on the bed, and then leaned against the headboard. "Is that a threat if I don't comply with your demands? I'm a grown ass man who's not tied down to anybody. I can do whatever I want, Stacee." Stacee slightly nodded. "Fine…I'ma start taking my weekends off from now on; the friend I was telling you about that has my old place…she's my girlfriend. And since you're not gonna go on a date tonight, after I put the boys back to bed again, when they wake up…I'ma go back to my place and fuck my girl." Stacee said nothing else, as he turned around and then walked out the bedroom. Michael sat there and then swallowed hard; he sighed and then rubbed his hands down his face. Michael then shook his head.

*   *   *

Jaquelyn had already made it to Dallas earlier and went to the store to stock up on supplies, while in disguise. She was on her way back to the lake house when she looked in the rearview mirror and saw a car following her; she didn't think anything of it, but every turn she made, the car behind her, did the same. Jaquelyn didn't want to be paranoid, but now was. She thought she was being followed and possibly by the police.

Jaquelyn sped up and so did the car, so she sped up even more. The car behind her, sped up as well and Jaquelyn was now scared. She kept looking in the rearview mirror and making sharp turns in the dead of the night. Jaquelyn was driving way too fast and not paying much attention to the road, while trying to figure out who was right on her bumper now.

Jaquelyn started to panic, as she reached the speed of over a hundred miles an hour. As she looked in the rearview mirror again, she looked for too long; Jaquelyn looked back at the road and it was too late…she screamed, as she flew off the road and then drove straight into a tree. The airbags deployed and hit Jaquelyn in the face; it knocked her out cold. The front of the car was completely mangled. The other car that was following Jaquelyn stopped by the side of the road; the passenger side window went down, and then Ricky looked out. He shook his head. "Scary ass bitch…that should of killed her, so let's get out of here." Shooter nodded and then drove from the side of the road, to leave.

Jaquelyn's body was still in the car, as smoke came from the mangled hood. Not too long after, a passerby drove by and then stopped; the man got out his car, and then hurried over to Jaquelyn's car. He saw that there was a woman inside, so immediately went into action, to get her out. He was able to pull Jaquelyn out the car in the nick of time; he dragged her away and then the car exploded. The impact sent the man and Jaquelyn's body flying to the ground. While on the ground, the man pulled his cellphone out his pocket and then called for an ambulance. Afterwards, he attempted to perform CPR on Jaquelyn, while he waited for emergency responders to arrive.

# Chapter 4

It was the end of the week, and everyone was thankful it was the weekend. Maxwell had gotten off early from work, and then went home to his twins. Angeline had the six-month-old twins playing on a mat on the floor. Allen was also in the living room and playing with the babies on the floor.

Maxwell walked in the living room and smiled. "Is everybody having fun?" Allen turned his head and then stood from the floor. "Sorry, Mr. Marshall…" Maxwell put his hand up and then dropped it. "No problem, Allen…" Maxwell walked over to the babies, and then picked up Madison; he sat down on the couch, with her. "Hey…hey, daddy's baby girl…" She smiled at him, and he smiled back. The staff in the house were happy when they were given the news of Maxwell having twins; the idea of having babies in the house made everyone happy, especially knowing that Maxwell had them with Jovanni. They knew her condition and made sure her twins were well taken care of while she was in a coma.

Maxwell handed Madison to Angeline, and then stood from the couch. "I'm gonna take a shower and then come back down." Angeline nodded and then Maxwell walked out the living room. Angeline and Allen went back to playing with the babies; after another fifteen minutes, the doorbell rang. Angeline frowned and then it continued to ring; when no response, banging on the door started.

Angeline laid Madison on the playmat, as Allen got up from the floor; he hurried out the living room to go to the front. When he reached the door, he opened it and then slightly stepped back; his mouth opened, and he couldn't close it. He then whispered to himself. "Ms. Jaquelyn…" Jaquelyn looked behind her and then stormed in the house; she closed the door behind her and then looked at Allen. "Where's Max?" Allen shook his head. "Uh, he's in the shower…" She nodded and then tried to run past Allen, but he stopped her. "No, you can't, Ms. Jaquelyn…you gotta leave now, before Mr. Marshall comes out and sees you." Jaquelyn frowned. "No, I can't leave…I need to find out what's going on." Before another word could be said, Maxwell walked to the front and then frowned, when he saw Jaquelyn. "What the fuck…what are you doing here? I'm calling the police." Maxwell turned around and then ran to the living room. Jaquelyn frowned and then ran after him; she almost slid on the floor, when she reached the living room. "No! What the fuck is going on, Max? I woke up in a hospital with cops outside my damn hospital room." Maxwell had his cellphone in his hand and was about to call the police, when he heard that; he slowly turned around to Jaquelyn and then stared at her. "You woke up where? What hospital?" Jaquelyn shook her head. "I don't know; it was named after the chicken…KFC." Allen interjected. "I think she means, KPC." Maxwell looked at Allen and then back to Jaquelyn. "Who are you?" Jaquelyn threw her hands up. "It's me, JoJo…so once again you can't tell us apart? Did you have me committed or something, since I was handcuffed to a damn bed, like a fucking mental patient."

Maxwell shook his head. "No…no, there's no fucking way this is possible again." He looked at Allen. "Call the hospital and see if JoJo is still there, and in a coma." Allen nodded and then ran over to the landline phone, while Jaquelyn frowned. "What the hell are you talking about? What do you mean I'm in a coma? They said I just got out of one…and they kept calling me Jaquelyn…" Jovanni stopped talking, and then realized something; she touched her hair and then sucked in air when she finally realized that it was short and not long.

Maxwell dropped his cellphone on the floor and then shook his head; shortly after, Allen went back over to Maxwell. "She's still there and in a coma, sir." Maxwell swallowed hard and then shook his head. "I'm calling the police now…JoJo is still in a coma and you're a wanted woman for stabbing her, so all I want is for you to rot in prison, where you belong. Allen, call the police." Jaquelyn shook her head, and then looked at Allen. "Allen, don't!" She looked at Maxwell. "Max, it's me…it's JoJo…" He shook his head, as he became emotional. "I can't fall for that again, Jaquelyn…please stop." Jaquelyn looked behind her and then back to Maxwell. "I'm on borrowed time here, Max…I escaped from the damn hospital, and I stole somebody's car, so what can I do or say for you to believe me? Ask me anything…please, just hurry up. I'm not Jaquelyn…I can't go to prison, Max!"

Maxwell rubbed both hands down his face, and then Angeline joined the guys; Jovanni looked at her. "Angeline…it's me, JoJo…" Angeline shook her head and then Maxwell spoke. "When was the first time we met?" Jaquelyn frowned. "Which damn time, when you grabbed me in that sports bar and said we had a relationship, or when Jaquelyn was in a damn coma and came out…" Jaquelyn stopped and then turned her head to the side; she looked back at Maxwell and then shook her head. "No…no, I'm in a coma? Jaquelyn was in a coma…it happened again? That's not possible, right? Max, that's not possible, right? I can't go to prison for stabbing myself!" Maxwell frowned, as he stared at her. "That's not good enough…and I can't think straight right now."

They heard sirens and Angeline looked at Allen, before looking back at Jaquelyn. "JoJo, what did I tell you about Mr. Marshall, when you first started coming over on weekends?" Maxwell looked at Angeline and frowned; Jaquelyn opened her mouth. "Uh, uh…you said he was damaged goods, but even lost souls can be found again; that he loved me and even though I looked like Jaquelyn, I was far from her and the best thing that happened to Max." Maxwell raised an eyebrow, and Angeline smiled. "It's her…word for word." Allen frowned, as banging was heard on the door. Jaquelyn turned her head, and then looked back at Maxwell. Before another word could be said, the door was broken in and everyone jumped.

The police had their guns drawn and told everyone to put their hands up; they all did, except for Jaquelyn. She turned to them, and then to Maxwell. "Max, I'm JoJo! I'm JoJo!" Jaquelyn was quickly grabbed and then turned around; handcuffs were put on her, as she continued to yell at Maxwell. "Max! We had a week left before I turned back into Jaquelyn…you were gonna take vacation time and we were supposed to go to Jamaica! You bought the tickets already! *Don't be mad about this shit…if I only got about a week left, then let's just spend that time together.* Remember, Max!" Maxwell frowned and then dropped his hands, as he stepped closer to her. "JoJo…wait, you can't take her!" Maxwell tried to run over to grab Jaquelyn, but Allen and Angeline quickly grabbed Maxwell. "No! Wait!" Jaquelyn yelled back. "Call Ricky and Randall!"

Maxwell was held back, as Jaquelyn was being dragged out the front door. After she was taken away, she could still be heard yelling. Maxwell shook his head and was almost traumatized. He looked at Allen. "This can't be real…I have to be dreaming…" Allen put his hand on Maxwell's shoulder. "Mr. Marshall…you better call Mr. Del Monte and Mr. Hepner; she's gonna need an attorney." Maxwell looked at him, and then nodded.

Angeline had returned to the living room to the twins. Maxwell ran to the living room, and then grabbed his cellphone from the floor, to make the call. He didn't explain anything in detail but told Ricky that they had to come to Dallas immediately, in regards to Jovanni. After his call, he told Allen and Angeline to watch the kids; that he would be back.

# Chapter 5

Maxwell was in his car, and on his way to the hospital; he had his cellphone on speaker, as he drove. It rang and then it was answered. "Hello…" Maxwell nodded. "Mike, have you been watching the news?" Michael frowned, as he walked in the living room. "Uh, no…for what?" Maxwell hit the steering wheel. "Did they find Jaquelyn?" Michael frowned again. "I don't know, Max, why?" Maxwell was getting frustrated. "Go to your office and look up Jaquelyn…hurry up!" Michael continued to frown and then walked out the living room. "Alright, I'm going…what's this about?" Maxwell continued to drive. "You wouldn't believe me if I told you…again." Michael shook his head, while in his office; he logged into his computer and then started to type. "Alright, I'm checking for you…and uh, yeah…it's right here. Jaquelyn was in a car accident. She crashed her car into a tree; she was taken by life flight and in a coma for two days. She woke up and then escaped from the hospital today. I swear that bitch is a lunatic…" Maxwell shook his head. "It's JoJo! She came to the house today and was dragged out by the cops…I swear, Mike…it's happening again; it was JoJo, and they took her."

Michael rose from the computer with a frown on his face. "That's impossible, Max…the first time that happened, was impossible. That can't happen a second time, right?" Maxwell shook his head. "I don't know, but Angeline questioned her, and JoJo got it right, then JoJo said something that only she would know. I'm on my way to the hospital now, where JoJo is at." Michael tried to keep up with everything that his brother was saying. "Wait a minute, Max, you're on the way to the hospital for what? What are you gonna do?" Maxwell punched the accelerator on the car. "I have to go wake up JoJo, or her personality is going to prison." Maxwell ended the call, as Michael frowned. "What? Hello…Max!" Michael took the cellphone from his ear and then cursed to himself. Michael ran out his office and then hurried to the stairs, to go upstairs and then grab his shoes; he was going to try to catch Maxwell at the hospital, before he made things worse.

*　*　*

Cyrus was at the hospital and with Nathan; he drove in town to see his niece. Cyrus had gotten off work early and then went home to check on Bernadine, before he went to the hospital. Cyrus was sitting next to Jovanni's bed, while Nathan stood; the men were talking, when they heard yelling coming from outside the door. Both turned their heads and frowned. Cyrus stood from the chair, as the door flew open. Maxwell ran in and then closed the door behind him; he leaned against the door, as the security tried to push it in. Cyrus frowned. "Max, what are you doing?" Maxwell shook his head, as he struggled to keep the door closed. "Mr. Mann…they arrested JoJo…" Cyrus frowned and then looked at his brother, as Nathan was equally confused. "Max, I know all this is taking a toll on you, but JoJo is right here." Maxwell shook his head. "No, it's happening again! She came to see me today and the cops took her…it was JoJo's personality again. Jaquelyn was in a car accident and in a coma for a couple of days; she just woke up…as JoJo! You have to believe me!" Nathan was speechless and then looked at his brother. The door was pushed in, and Maxwell was flung away from it.

Maxwell ran over to the bed and then grabbed Jovanni's body. "Wake up! JoJo, wake up, baby!" Cyrus grabbed Maxwell, as well as the security when they ran over to help. "Max, calm down!" Maxwell was dragged back from the bed. "JoJo's in jail! Wake her body up! She's in jail!" Michael ran in the room and then hurried over to his brother. "Let him go…he's not crazy!" Cyrus put his hands up to the security. "Let him go, please! He's her husband and he's grieving! It's alright!" The security slowly let Maxwell go, and then Michael grabbed his brother and held him.

Cyrus looked at Maxwell and then to the security. "Please…it's alright…his wife been in a coma for two months; he's just not taking it good. We're good…" The security nodded and then they left, along with the nurses that were behind them. Nathan looked at

Maxwell. "Are you trying to get yourself arrested or thrown in the looney bin?" Maxwell shook his head. "It's JoJo…it happened like it did before. I swear, I'm telling the truth…Nathan, she told you, she told you about us…I know she did. You said it wasn't possible, but since she and Jaquelyn were twins, then maybe it was. Regardless, it happened again… JoJo's personality in Jaquelyn's body, was just arrested at my damn house. We need to wake up JoJo's body now." Michael sighed, as he turned his head to Cyrus and Nathan, who were both in disbelief of what they were hearing.

Cyrus shook his head. "I don't know what I'm supposed to say to that…" Nathan frowned. "That can't be…I mean…" Michael interjected. "I looked it up…Jaquelyn was in a car accident and in the hospital; she was in a coma for a couple of days and woke up today. She escaped from the hospital and apparently went to Max, not knowing what was going on. I wasn't there, so I don't know if it was her or not." Maxwell shot his brother a look. "Angeline and Allen were there…Angeline asked her a question; I couldn't think straight to ask anything right. Her last words to me…Jaquelyn wouldn't know that…only JoJo. It was her and she's in jail now…we have to wake JoJo's body up now."

Nathan shook his head and then sighed. "Max, let's say that everything you just said is true…we can't wake up a comatose body for the hell of it. And nobody is gonna believe that story; we barely believed it, the first time around. Now you want us to believe that it happened again?" Maxwell sighed and then nodded. "JoJo told me to call Ricky and Randall, so I called them after she was taken; they won't believe this either, but all they have to do…is ask her questions. Jaquelyn spent no time with Ricky and definitely not Randall, so if she can answer any questions that they have, right…will you believe it then?" Nathan looked at Cyrus and then back to Maxwell.

Nathan slowly nodded his head. "If she answers every question right, then I'll believe it, but it's still unbelievable and not sane. This can't be real, but I'll believe it after they see her and confirm." Cyrus rubbed his hands down his face, and then sighed; he looked at Maxwell. "I'll believe it too…" Maxwell nodded and was relieved. Michael said they should go. Maxwell nodded and then walked over to Jovanni's body; he leaned in to her and then kissed her on the forehead. Maxwell slightly pulled up from her and then smiled. "Baby, if you're in there…please wake up. You're in the wrong place again, and I need you to wake up and come back to me, the right way."

Maxwell rose from Jovanni and then looked at the men, before looking at his brother; he nodded to him and then both walked out the room, after telling Cyrus and Nathan goodbye. After they left, Nathan put his hand over his face and Cyrus shook his head. "I so much wanna believe him, just so I can talk to my daughter again, but it can't be true…not again, right?" Cyrus looked at Nathan, who looked back at him. "The better question is…if JoJo is in Jaquelyn's body, then who is in this body?" Both turned to look at Jovanni, who was lying there peacefully.

# Chapter 6

Michael went home, after coming from his brother's house; after they left the hospital, Michael followed his brother back to his house to stay with him and calm him down. He was anxious for Randall and Ricky to get in town, so he could speak to them, after they spoke to Jovanni. They weren't coming until the next day, so Maxwell had to wait. Michael helped his brother get the twins situated and then gave Maxwell something to go to sleep, because he hadn't been getting much rest since Jovanni went into a coma. Angeline cared for the twins in the middle of the night.

It was close to eleven, when Michael arrived home; he hung his keys on the wall and then sighed, as he made his way through the house and then to the stairs. Before he reached the stairs, Stacee stopped him. "I told you I had somewhere to be tonight, Mike. You said you were gonna be back in a little bit, but that was hours ago." Michael stopped and then looked at Stacee. "I'm tired and I had a long day and now night; you said you were going to see your girlfriend, so go now…you have the whole weekend." Michael started to go up the stairs, as he rubbed his hand down his face. Stacee sucked his teeth, and then followed him.

Once upstairs, Michael walked to his bedroom and then went inside; he left the door open, since he thought Stacee was leaving. Stacee walked in the bedroom and then stopped. "Mike…" Michael turned around to Stacee, and then sat down on the bed, to take his shoes off. "What?" Stacee turned his head to the side and then back to Michael. "I told you I never been with a guy before." Michael frowned, as he stared at Stacee. "Uh, ok…" Stacee sighed. "I want to…so what can I do to make that happen?" Michael was confused, more so, since he was tired. "I'm sorry, what? What are we talking about…is that a riddle?" Stacee rolled his eyes. "I been practicing, well preparing for about a couple of weeks…so that can happen." Michael stared at Stacee with a blank look on his face. "You've been practicing fucking men for a couple of weeks, so you can make what happen? So, you can fuck more men? Help me out here, Stacee, because I'm tired and as you can see, I'm confused."

Stacee walked over to Michael, and then stopped in front of him; he felt he should stop beating around the bush and get straight to the point. "I wanna be with you…in that way, so I bought something from one of them sex shops a couple of weeks ago, and used it on myself, so it wouldn't seem like I was a virgin when I decided to be with a guy…if you get what I'm saying." Michael slowly nodded his head and understood now. "Oh…wow, ok. Yeah, I get what you're saying now." Stacee nodded his head, as Michael stood from the bed; he eyed Stacee. "I thought you had somewhere to be tonight…for the weekend." Stacee cleared his throat. "I do, and I still can be if you don't want anything from me." Michael slightly nodded his head. "Are the boys asleep?" Stacee nodded. "I just put them down before you came in." Michael nodded and then stepped back a little from Stacee; he removed his shirt and then flung it to the floor. "I'm not that tired anymore…" Stacee grinned, and then stepped closer to Michael; they started to kiss hard and then Stacee dropped his keys on the floor, to grab Michael.

Stacee moved them back to the bed, and then they both fell back on it. They continued to kiss hard, and then Stacee was in between Michael's legs. It would be their first time together and something that both had been wanting for some time. It was also Stacee's first-time having sex with a man, so with Michael's experience, Stacee hoped that he met Michael's expectations.

# Chapter 7

It was the next day, and Maxwell couldn't wait to get up. He called Ricky and asked if they were in town yet. Ricky said they were on the road and on their way. Maxwell got himself together in the bathroom, and then went downstairs; he went to the living room and then walked in to see the twins, with Angeline. Jax was in the swing with his bottle, while Angeline was feeding Madison.

Maxwell looked at Jax, and then raised an eyebrow. "Is he holding his own bottle?" Angeline looked at Jax and then to Maxwell; she smiled and then nodded. "Yes, Mr. Marshall…that boy was tired of waiting for me." Maxwell slightly laughed, and then shook his head; he went over to Jax and then smiled. "Hey lil' man…you're acting just like your Uncle Mike now; he's more impatient than me."

Angeline shook her head, as she fed Madison and then opened her mouth, after she let the bottle go. "Mr. Marshall…" Maxwell turned his head, and then saw Madison holding her own bottle now. Angeline slightly laughed. "They're already competing with each other, Mr. Marshall…" He shook his head. "I see…yep, more like me and Mike every day." They both slightly laughed, and then the doorbell rang. Maxwell sat down on the couch, while Allen went to the door.

Shortly after, Allen entered the living room and had Ricky and Randall behind him. Maxwell turned his head, after they entered, and then stood from the couch. "I'm glad you're here…you two can follow me to the den." Ricky nodded and then Maxwell walked out the living room; the men followed him.

Once in the den, they all sat down and Randall yawned, since they got up so early. Maxwell sighed. "Jaquelyn was here yesterday…but it wasn't her, it was JoJo." Ricky frowned and then looked at Randall, before looking back at Maxwell. "What? JoJo still in a coma, right?" Maxwell slightly nodded his head. "Uh yeah, but the thing is…I know you're not gonna believe this, but did JoJo ever tell you the story of how we met?" The men looked at each other, and then back to Maxwell; both shook their heads no. Maxwell nodded and then cleared his throat. "Look, I know this is gonna sound crazy, but it's true and many can verify that this is true." Ricky was confused. "What the fuck you talkin' about? Did y'all meet in outer space or something?" Randall slightly laughed, and then Maxwell sighed. "No…when I was married to Jaquelyn, she was in a car accident; she was in a coma for a year. When she woke up, she wasn't herself…it was like she was somebody else; everybody noticed the change in her, even me. She didn't talk the same, dress the same, or anything…" Randall frowned. "What's your point? That happens sometimes." Maxwell shook his head. "She woke up and told everybody to call her…JoJo." Ricky frowned, and then looked at Randall; he looked back at Maxwell. "JoJo? That don't mean nothing…she was tryin' to be her sister again, like she did with you."

Maxwell shook his head. "Jaquelyn and JoJo hadn't met yet…they didn't know about each other; nobody knew…the point is, I fell in love with a personality that was in the wrong body. When Jaquelyn came back, she was her old self, and my brother had to convince me to move on. Well, the following year, I was in Houston for work and at a sports bar…I saw Jaquelyn, well a woman that looked just like her: it was JoJo. I called her that and she responded. I tried to explain to her what happened and who I was, but she didn't believe me. It was later confirmed that at the time that Jaquelyn was in her coma, JoJo was in a coma too, at the same time. JoJo had an allergic reaction to anesthesia, just like now…she was in a coma for a month, the same amount of time that her personality was with me, here. She woke up from her coma in Houston and that's when Jaquelyn's personality came back here." Ricky and Randall stared at Maxwell, as if he lost his mind; Randall had no words and was just dumbfounded.

Ricky frowned. "So, you saying that JoJo woke up in Jaquelyn's body, again?" Maxwell nodded and Ricky continued. "Then who the fuck in JoJo's body?" Randall looked at Ricky and frowned. "Are you seriously entertaining this?" Ricky looked at Randall, and then rolled his eyes. Maxwell interjected. "It's true…" They both looked at him again, as he continued. "Cyrus can confirm it and so can all her friends and family…Nathan put her in a medically induced coma again, so she could remember me and what we had; it worked, and she did remember. I know this all sounds crazy, but it happened again. Both were in a coma again, and JoJo woke up in Jaquelyn's body; she came here after waking up from a coma and escaping from the hospital. The cops took her, and she told me to call you two…I went to the hospital where JoJo's body is, and I tried to convince Cyrus and Nathan that this was happening again. Nobody believes this is possible, so you have to help JoJo."

Ricky was about to speak, when Randall did. "Jaquelyn is in jail right now for stabbing JoJo, so she's where she belongs." Maxwell shook his head and then abruptly stood from the couch. "That's not Jaquelyn…it's JoJo and you can't let her go to prison, at least not until JoJo wakes up in her own body, so everything can go back to normal." Randall frowned. "Normal? Nothing you just said sounds normal…" Maxwell put his hand over his face, and then Randall nodded; he stood from the couch. "Let's just say I believe you for one minute…what exactly do you want me to do?"

Maxwell looked at Randall and then sighed. "If you don't believe all this, then it's useless…" Ricky looked at Randall, and then back to Maxwell. "How we supposed to believe something like this?" Maxwell looked at Ricky. "All you have to do is ask questions…ask Jaquelyn, well JoJo, questions that only she would know. Jaquelyn spent no time with you or Randall…so ask her questions that only JoJo would know. After you're convinced, we have to keep JoJo out of jail or bail her out or something, until her body wakes up."

Ricky stood from the couch, and then cleared his throat; he thought for a moment and then shook his head. "Nah…we not gonna do that." Both looked at Ricky, as he rubbed his chin with his hand; he then looked between the men. "If you say that Jaquelyn is really JoJo right now, then that's the best shit…" Randall frowned. "How?" Ricky grinned. "Have JoJo plead guilty to everything…so when she wakes up from her coma, JoJo is out, and Jaquelyn won't know what the fuck hit her. She'd be in prison, and it'd be too late for her…she won't remember what happened or why she's in there. You gonna be her attorney, so nobody can say she ain't have one." Randall frowned, and Maxwell thought that was a good idea. "That…that actually sounds like a great plan." Maxwell frowned and slightly shook his head, since he couldn't believe he didn't think of it.

Randall sighed and then nodded. "Can we just wait and see first if all this is true, before planning a damn scheme like that?" Ricky looked at him, and then nodded. Ricky looked back at Maxwell. "Alright…we're gonna go see her." Maxwell nodded and then told both men where she was. The men nodded and then afterwards, Maxwell walked them out, so they could go see Jaquelyn.

# Chapter 8

Jaquelyn was sitting in a visiting section of the jail; she was sitting on a bench on one side and then she looked up to see Ricky and Randall coming her way. Jaquelyn slightly nodded when they reached her. Randall cleared his throat and then sat down with Ricky on the opposite side. Seeing Jaquelyn with her cut hair and wounds on her face, from the car accident, made Ricky cringe; he once again went back to not believing this was true, and maybe a set up.

Randall looked at Ricky, and then back to Jaquelyn; neither had said a word yet, while not knowing where to begin. Jaquelyn looked between both of them. "Are y'all gonna say something? Did Max, tell y'all what was going on?" The men looked at each other, and then back to Jaquelyn. Ricky sighed. "How we know who you really are?" Jaquelyn sighed. "It's me, Ricky…it's JoJo." Ricky shook his head. "Nah, this shit is twisted…I don't believe this shit." Jaquelyn rolled her eyes, as Randall spoke, but his words weren't aimed at anyone. "Just ask questions…" Ricky looked at him. "What?" Randall looked at him, and then back to Jaquelyn. "What's Shooter's real name?" Ricky looked at Randall, and then back to Jaquelyn; she sighed. "Steven…" Ricky slightly nodded his head. "Good guess…" Randall looked at him and frowned, as Ricky continued. "Which one of my associates did you fuck?" Randall shot Ricky a look, and Jaquelyn rolled her eyes. "Me and Shooter never fucked…we just kissed; you know nothing else happened…" Randall frowned. "What?" Ricky put his hand up to his dad, as he continued to stare at Jaquelyn. "How much was Max sending you every two months for child support?" Jaquelyn frowned. "Really, Ricky…? He sent me money every two weeks, fifteen hundred dollars…" Randall raised an eyebrow. "Really? That much, every two damn weeks? What type of child support payment is that?" Ricky looked at Randall and frowned. "Shut up…" He looked back at Jaquelyn. "You gotta know that this shit is like impossible, right?" Jaquelyn sighed and then nodded. "I already did my time in jail, Ricky…I can't be here again, unless this is punishment for what Randall did by paying that fucking judge off and pleading me out. I knew this shit would come back on me." Randall frowned. "You wanted to be free, didn't you, so I got you…" Ricky interjected. "Wait a minute…Jaquelyn wouldn't know that shit…only JoJo."

The men looked at each other, and then back to Jaquelyn. Ricky shook his head. "Ok, you got our attention, and we might believe you. So, what you gonna have to do is plead guilty to everything, so when your body wakes up, Jaquelyn will be in prison and you'll be out with Max." Jaquelyn sighed, and then sucked her teeth. "How long?" Randall raised an eyebrow. "Well, I'm convinced now…" Ricky rolled his eyes, and then Jaquelyn rubbed her hands down her face. "This is a fucking nightmare…what are the damn odds that bitch Jaquelyn would get in another car accident; I swear she can't drive or something." Ricky looked at Randall, and then back to Jaquelyn. "Uh, JoJo…maybe this might be my fault." Jaquelyn raised an eyebrow. "What are you trying to say?" Ricky sighed. "Me and Shooter made Jaquelyn run off the road…she crashed into a tree, and we left her; we thought she was dead, but somebody must of came by and helped her."

Randall put his hand over his face, as Jaquelyn stared at Ricky. "You did this? Well thanks a lot, Ricky…I woke up handcuffed to a hospital bed with armed cops outside my door." Randall frowned. "How did you escape?" Jaquelyn cleared her throat. "After the nurse called me Jaquelyn and told me that the cops were gonna take me to jail, I got mad…so after she left, a cop came in and then unhandcuffed me. I had a hospital gown on, so don't ask what I let the cop see…" Ricky frowned, as Randall shook his head. Jaquelyn sucked her teeth. "The point is, he was distracted, so I grabbed his gun and told him to lay down, or I was gonna shoot him. He did what I said and then I grabbed my clothes before I ran out with the gun. I threw the gun in the parking lot and stole a car on the way out…" Randall put his hand up to stop her. "Hold on…you pulled a gun on a cop, and stole a car, to go along with the already charges that Jaquelyn is already facing for being on the run?" Jaquelyn slightly nodded her head, and Ricky made a sarcastic sound. "All you had to do was tell that story first, and I would of believed you…Jaquelyn nothing but a scary ass bitch, so I know she couldn't of pulled all that off." Randall rolled his eyes, as Jaquelyn sighed. Ricky continued. "Look, JoJo…Max said you gotta wake up, for this all to get back right."

Jaquelyn slightly nodded her head. "The first time…it lasted about a month." The guys looked at each other and then back to her. Randall nodded. "Can you make it that long?" Jaquelyn swallowed hard and then cleared her throat; she was becoming emotional, but didn't want to break down, especially not in front of them. "Yeah, I guess…" Ricky sighed, as he stared at her. "JoJo…I know what I always say to you and Shooter, about being weak, but I already told you that you not weak. It's cool if this shit hittin' you hard and you gotta let it out. You been through a lot already…" Jaquelyn slightly nodded her head; her facial expression didn't change, but a few tears did run down her face. "Yeah, I know, but I'm good…I did this before, so I can handle it again. Just plead guilty to everything, right? And y'all are sure this'll work?" Ricky sighed and then looked at Randall; he looked at Ricky and then back to Jaquelyn. "If everything you and Max said was true, then the last thing you want is for Jaquelyn to get off these charges. You want her in here and to stay locked up for good. When you woke up from your coma, is when you went back to your own body, right?"

Jaquelyn nodded, and Ricky rubbed his hands down his face. Randall nodded. "Ok, so that's what we're gonna do. I'm gonna talk to the District Attorney and take care of this." Jaquelyn nodded. "Yeah, alright..." Both nodded and then stood from the bench. She looked at them and then sighed, as they told her goodbye. They walked away from the table, and she hoped that she would make it.

After leaving the jail, Randall made a few calls, while Ricky made some of his own. Ricky called Maxwell and informed him that they believed the story after speaking to Jaquelyn. He informed Maxwell of their next move, and Maxwell agreed to it. Maxwell called Cyrus and the news went on from there, after Maxwell called his brother as well. Maxwell had to mentally get himself together to make it through this and go see Jaquelyn in jail.

# Chapter 9

It was the next day, and Cyrus was depressed; he went home to Bernadine and had to inform her of the unbelievable story of how Maxwell and Jovanni met, today. Not too many people knew the backstory, especially no one in Maxwell's family, except for Michael.

Cyrus was sitting on the couch and had just told Bernadine the entire story; she had her hand on her stomach and her mouth open the entire time she listened to Cyrus. When he was done, Bernadine was dumbfounded. "Uh, wow…and everyone believes this?" Cyrus sighed and then nodded. "It's nothing to believe, baby…it's the truth and it's happening again. They're identical twins…I know it all sounds crazy, but JoJo is in jail right now in Jaquelyn's body, and JoJo's body is in a coma on a bed, in a hospital." Bernadine sighed and then nodded. "Ok, I believe you…you look scared, and I know you wouldn't make something like this up. What can I do?"

Cyrus rubbed his hands down his face, and then shook his head. "There's nothing you can do…there's nothing I can do. We gotta play this out and hope for the best." Bernadine nodded and then Cyrus's cellphone rang; he grabbed it from the coffee table and saw it was Nathan, so he answered. "Hey, Nate…"

Nathan cleared his throat, as he stood in the men's restroom. "Cyrus…get down here now." Cyrus frowned and then looked at Bernadine, as he continued to speak. "What? Why?" What's going on?" Nathan shook his head. "She woke up…" Cyrus smiled and then stood from the couch. "JoJo woke up? Really, Nate? That's good news, I'ma…" Nathan interjected. "No, Cyrus…JoJo didn't wake up…Jaquelyn did." Cyrus frowned. "What the hell do you mean, Jaquelyn woke up? How do you know it's Jaquelyn and not JoJo?" Nathan sighed, as he looked around. "They said it was amnesia, but I know it's not…she talked like Jaquelyn and was confused about how she got in the hospital. She asked if she was going to jail for what she did to JoJo."

Cyrus put his hand to his face, and then dropped it. "No, no, Nate…that's not how it happened the first time, right? They both woke up in their own bodies, right?" Nathan sighed and then nodded. "That's what happened the first time, but I can't explain why it's happening like this now. I tried to get the nurses to stop calling her JoJo, but they wouldn't and then kicked me out the room. If Jaquelyn finds out that JoJo is really in jail, then she's gonna do everything in her power to keep JoJo's personality there and stay in JoJo's body, as a free woman." Cyrus couldn't believe this was happening. "I, I…tell me what to do, Nate…Max called me and said they could get JoJo to plead guilty to everything, so when her body woke up, she would be free, and Jaquelyn would be in prison already. This is bad…"

Nathan sighed and then shook his head. "I'm still here at the hospital, so maybe we just need to come up with a plan to keep Jaquelyn close. She can go stay with you and Bernadine…until they switch back and you can just act like she's really JoJo." Cyrus frowned, with confusion. "What?" Nathan rolled his eyes. "We can't let Jaquelyn out of our sight…because if she figures this out on her own, then she and JoJo will never go back to their own bodies, and JoJo will stay in jail." Cyrus put his hand over his face and then dropped it; he nodded. "Yeah, alright…just stay there and see when they're gonna release her, so you can bring her here." Nathan nodded. "Yeah, alright…I'll do that." Cyrus nodded and then both ended the call.

Nathan put his cellphone in his back pocket, and then walked out the men's restroom. He made his way down the hall and back to Jovanni's room; when he reached the room, he walked in and then frowned, when he didn't see Jovanni. Nathan walked all the way in the room and then looked around; he then walked back out the room and called for a nurse. A nurse walked over to him, as he spoke. "Where is Jovanni Mann?" The nurse looked inside and then slightly frowned; she looked back at Nathan. "She was in here…" Nathan put his hand over his face, and then dropped it. "What did she say…did she say anything about leaving?" The nurse shook her head. "She kept saying her name was Jaquelyn and not JoJo…or something like that. We had to explain to her what was going on and why she was there; she acted like she saw a ghost and then we left out the room. I don't know where she went." Nathan cursed to himself; he ran out the room, down the hall, and then all the way out the hospital.

*　*　*

Michael was at home and sitting on the couch; he was thinking about his conversation with his brother. Stacee walked into the living room and then stopped. "I thought you were at work?" Michael looked up at Stacee and then nodded. "Uh yeah, I was…I left and came home. Max is at home and didn't go in today." Stacee slightly nodded his head, as he walked over to Michael. "Alright, well what's going on?" Michael rubbed his hands down his face and then sighed. "You wouldn't believe me if I told you…" Before Stacee could respond, Michael's cellphone rang; it was on the coffee table, so Stacee glanced at it and then looked at Michael. "Aubrey, huh? I didn't know y'all were talking after he used your house to hide." Michael sighed, as he looked at Stacee. He continued to let his cellphone ring, as Stacee raised an eyebrow. Michael cleared his throat. "I called him on my way home, but he didn't answer." Stacee slightly nodded his head. "How come you're not answering now?" Michael looked at him. "I can call him back." Stacee made a sarcastic sound. "Right…" He was about to walk out the living room, when Michael spoke. "Do you have a problem with something?" Stacee looked back at him and then shook his head. "I don't have a problem with shit...you?" Michael rolled his eyes. "Well, I can see where this is going...you're jealous." Michael stood from the couch, as Stacee frowned. "Jealous of who...Aubrey? Damn...you're a conceited, vain, and arrogant ass guy." Michael frowned. "Conceited, vain, and arrogant? Those are big words, Stacee...have you been reading the dictionary lately?"

Stacee slightly nodded his head, as he stared at Michael. "Ok, that's what we're doing now? No, I didn't read the dictionary. I got all those big words from all your exes, when they were describing you." Michael gave Stacee a snide look, as Stacee smiled. Michael walked over to Stacee and then eyed him. "I called him to talk about JoJo...she's his friend. I'm not interested in Aubrey anymore...that's the past and maybe one day we can be friends again, but whether that happens or not, I don't want him back." Stacee slightly shrugged his shoulders. "Whatever...if that was true then you would of answered his call, in front of me." Michael sighed. "You had my attention and was talking to me, so I didn't wanna be rude, by answering his call in the middle of our conversation." Stacee turned his head to the side and then sighed.

Michael told Stacee to look at him, and he did. Michael then sighed. "We didn't confirm or make anything official, but in case you didn't notice...I stopped all my one-nighters with other men and women, and I've been spending my time with you and the boys, only. You're also the only one that's been in my bed every night, since the first time we were together. We don't have to label this if you don't want to…but know that I'm not interested in anybody else, not even Aubrey." Stacee sighed and then nodded. "Yeah, alright…well regardless, it don't matter, Mike…I'm still getting paid to do a job and I do it, so as long as I still got the label of your nanny, then I guess I can't be anything else to you anyway." Stacee said nothing else, as he walked away from Michael. Michael watched him leave and then sighed; he walked out the living room too and then went upstairs to take a shower.

# Chapter 10

Later that night, Maxwell was at his home and with his twins; the doorbell rang, and Allen went to the door. Shortly after, Allen brought the guests to the living room. Maxwell turned his head and then saw Ricky and Randall. Maxwell sighed and then dismissed Allen. After he walked out the living room, the guys went over to the couch and then sat down. Maxwell had a sorrowful look on his face.

Ricky looked at Randall and then back to Maxwell. "What's wrong with you?" Maxwell sighed and then shook his head. "We have a problem…" Randall raised an eyebrow. "What problem?" Maxwell set Jax on the floor, so he could play and then looked back at the men. "Cyrus called me…JoJo woke up." Ricky smiled and then nodded. "That's good…Randall already sealed the deal with the D.A. so Jaquelyn not getting out for a long time."

Maxwell's eyes became watery, and Randall frowned. Maxwell swallowed hard. "Jaquelyn woke up, not JoJo…then she took off from the hospital before they released her; she figured it out, from what Nathan told Cyrus." Ricky and Randall looked at each other and then back to Maxwell. Ricky slightly shook his head. "So, wait a minute, if Jaquelyn woke up in JoJo's body, then that means…" Randall interjected. "That JoJo is in jail, and not getting out for a long time." Ricky shot him a look and then frowned, before he looked back at Maxwell; he abruptly stood from the couch. "Ah hell nah! Make them switch back!" Maxwell stared at Ricky and then shook his head. "This didn't happen the first time…I don't know what's happening now or why, but I don't know how they can change back, if both are awake and not in a coma." Ricky rubbed his hands down his face, and then sat back down.

Randall shook his head. "This has to be the most insane thing I ever been involved in…" Ricky looked at him. "You can't change the deal?" Randall looked at him and frowned. "And do what, give Jaquelyn a defense? Everything's been taken care of already. I had to call in a lot of favors for this…this was your damn idea, not mine." Ricky sighed and then sat back against the couch. Maxwell shook his head. "Jaquelyn is missing…again, but in JoJo's body this time. There's no telling where she is now or what she'd do, since she's a free woman and can go anywhere." Ricky slightly nodded his head. "Well, I already know she ain't gonna stick around here…she can't be herself no more if everybody think she's in jail, so she's gonna have to pretend to be JoJo. But since we know what's going on already, and she don't know that we know…we got a damn advantage. We find her and then keep her ass locked up, until they switch back." Randall frowned, as he looked at his son. "So, now you're adding kidnapping and unlawful imprisonment charges to your resume?" Ricky looked at Randall and gave him a snide look. "Well, she might come back and be with Max…" Maxwell frowned and then shook his head. "No…I can't…I'm not letting her around my babies or in this house again. Maybe we can get rid of her…" Both shot Maxwell a look and frowned.

Randall put his hand up and then stood from the couch. "No…I don't think you're thinking too straight, right now. You can't get rid of JoJo's body…when her personality is in jail in Jaquelyn's body. You're either gonna kill JoJo for good, and Jaquelyn is in prison for life, or you're gonna kill Jaquelyn, and JoJo is in prison for life. You can't take that chance of messing this up…and I can't believe I just said all that." Randall put his hand over his face, as Ricky sighed.

Maxwell was distraught and didn't know what to think. "Well, what do we do?!" Randall removed his hand and then looked at Maxwell, as Ricky looked at him too. "You said Nathan put JoJo back in a coma, so she could remember you, right?" Maxwell nodded, and so did Ricky. "Alright, well put Jaquelyn in a coma…put them both in a coma again and then wait." Randall frowned, as he stared at Ricky. "Are you serious? JoJo's body just came out of a damn coma…" Maxwell shook his head. "No, he's right…this was the fourth time that JoJo's been in a coma…she might not be able to make it through another one. Maybe we can hit JoJo in the head or something." Ricky rolled his eyes and then stood from the couch. "That shit is more stupid than what I just said..." Maxwell rolled his eyes and then Randall interjected. "Look, all we have to do is make Jaquelyn believe that we don't know who she really is...we find her and make her think that we believe she's JoJo. At least until we think of something. All her friends have to be informed, so they'll be ready if she goes to see them. Tell Cyrus and anybody that JoJo knows, of what we all need to do." Maxwell sighed and then nodded. "Well, she was living with you, Ricky, so let her keep living with you...I'll keep my kids, and you come up with whatever lie you want, to explain that shit to her...why I have the twins, and she doesn't." Ricky frowned and then sucked his teeth. "Damn...alright, if she come my way, then I'll let her stay." Maxwell nodded and then before the guys left, Randall cleared his throat. "Uh, so which one of y'all is gonna tell JoJo that Jaquelyn woke up in her body and took off?" Maxwell opened his mouth, and then shook his head no. Ricky put both hands up and then shook his head too. "You her damn attorney, so you do it...I ain't in that shit. I already got volunteered to keep Jaquelyn at the house with me, so you gotta tell JoJo about this." Randall rolled his eyes and was dreading that conversation. "Fine...I'm doing this tomorrow, so we can head back to Houston after." Maxwell sighed. "You two can stay the night here, if you want." Randall nodded and then sat back down. "Yeah...sure." Ricky went over to Madison, and then picked her up; it had been some time since he had seen her. Randall went ahead and played with his great-grandson, while Maxwell sat back on the couch and was in deep thought.

# Chapter 11

It was a week later, and what started as great news that Jaquelyn had been arrested, turned into chaos overnight. Michael had called Aubrey back, after he was called again from Maxwell; the story was incredible, but once again it was taken seriously. Cyrus and everyone else, that was associated with Jovanni, in Dallas, knew the situation and what to do. Randall went to see Jaquelyn in jail the next morning and the meeting with her wasn't good. She was angry and sad at the same time and let her emotions out with the thought of never being free again or seeing her twins again. Randall hated to deliver this news, but it had to be done. All she could do now, was wait. Aubrey hadn't been able to get everyone together, but was able to, this time. He called a meeting, and he was waiting for everyone at his apartment.

*   *   *

There was a knock on the door, and Aubrey stood from the couch; he walked to the door and then opened it. He nodded to Auston and then stepped aside, so he could walk in; Deon and Desiray were right behind, then Mariya and Trey were next. Aubrey closed the door, and then Deon sat down on the couch; he was in his work uniform. "I had to leave work early, man, so this better be good." Trey looked at Aubrey. "Why are we having a damn meeting, Aubrey?" Aubrey walked around the couch and then stood there, as everyone sat down and then looked at him. Aubrey sighed. "That shit that happened with JoJo waking up from her coma, in Jaquelyn's body…it's happening again." Desiray frowned, as she looked at Mariya. Trey raised an eyebrow. "What the fuck are you talking about?"

Aubrey slightly threw his hands up. "Mike called me…JoJo's personality is in jail right now…and Jaquelyn woke up in JoJo's body last week; Nate confirmed it because he was at the hospital when JoJo, well Jaquelyn woke up. She was confused and told the nurses to stop calling her JoJo, because she was Jaquelyn. Once they kept feeding her info on what happened to her, Jaquelyn figured it out and then took off. So, what Max and everybody wants us to do, is if we see JoJo, then know it's not her…and really Jaquelyn. We pretend like it's really JoJo, so Jaquelyn won't get suspicious and try to run again. That's the only way to keep Jaquelyn around, until they can switch back." They all frowned, as they stared at Aubrey. Trey shook his head and then slightly looked down. Deon frowned. "So, wait a minute…that shit didn't happen last time, so why it happen like that now?" Aubrey shrugged his shoulders. "I don't know, man…" Desiray interjected. "What's gonna happen to JoJo?" Aubrey looked at her. "Before JoJo woke up…she was told by Randall and Ricky to plead guilty to everything, so when she woke back up, they would switch back and JoJo would be free, and Jaquelyn would be in prison for life. JoJo woke up after that deal was made, but they didn't switch back, like they thought. So, JoJo is really in jail now and going to prison, and Jaquelyn is free until they can switch back." Auston frowned and Mariya shook her head. "I'm so fucking confused…" Desiray rolled her eyes and Deon sighed; he lit a cigarette, as Trey swallowed hard. "She…she's at the apartment." Everyone looked at Trey, as he looked up at everybody. Aubrey frowned. "What do you mean, she's at the apartment?"

Trey sighed and then shook his head. "She came to the apartment a few days ago and said she got into some shit with Max; she asked if she could stay with me for a while and I said, yeah…" Deon rolled his eyes, as Auston put his hand over his face. Desiray was in disbelief. "So, you wasn't even gonna tell us that she was out of the coma?" Trey sucked his teeth. "She didn't want nobody to know." Desiray frowned, as Aubrey shook his head. "And she used those words to tell you that?" Trey slightly shrugged his shoulders. "She didn't sound right, but you already know that Jaquelyn got her hair cut and JoJo's is long, so when I saw the long hair and she said she was JoJo, I didn't think nothing of it. It's your fault, Aubrey…you knew this shit last week, so you should of said something." Deon laughed, as smoke came out his mouth.

Aubrey gave him a snide look. "I can't keep up with y'all niggas…I been trying to get everybody together since I found out, so I can only explain this shit one time." Auston sighed and then sat back against the couch. Desiray nodded her head. "Alright, well keep her at the apartment with you and call Mike back; tell him where she's at, and then let Ricky or Randall take it from there, 'cause this shit is way over our heads." Deon nodded and had to agree.

Trey cleared his throat. "There's something else…" Aubrey looked at his brother, and then raised an eyebrow. "What?" Trey sighed. "She's been trying to fuck since she got there." Desiray frowned and Mariya shook her head. Deon looked at his brother. "Well, that should of been your first sign, that she wasn't JoJo…" Auston laughed, as the others joined him. Trey rolled his eyes. "Y'all shut up…I know now what the deal is, but…I mean, it's JoJo's body and that before so…" Mariya shook her head while in disgust. "That's some sick shit…" Trey frowned, as he looked at her. "So, Max could fuck JoJo, when she was in Jaquelyn's body, but I can't do it?" Aubrey frowned. "They were married at the time…Jaquelyn was his wife, so it don't matter if he fucked his wife's body." Desiray interjected. "He's right, Trey…you can't; if JoJo do get her body back, she's gonna fuck you up, or Max for taking advantage of her." Trey rolled his eyes. "Uh, JoJo used to be my wife too…it's not like we never fucked before." Auston interjected. "Dude, why are you still talking about this?" Trey turned his head away and Deon frowned; he slowly shook his head. "Nigga…you already did it, didn't you? You already fucked her, didn't you?" Desiray's jaw dropped and Aubrey put his hand over his face. Mariya cleared her throat. "Wow, Trey…" Trey sighed. "Yeah, I did, but if it makes y'all feel better, it wasn't all it was cracked up to be. I guess I know why now…Jaquelyn is damn near a virgin, since her experience is limited. It felt like I was in junior high, having sex for the first time. The shit was just all wrong, and she didn't know what the fuck she was doing. She let out this howling sound, when she 'came', and I thought I was in a horror movie."

Auston fell off the couch, while laughing hard, while the others followed his lead. Aubrey shook his head, as he laughed, and Trey found nothing funny. "Y'all shut up…" Desiray spoke in between laughs. "That's what you get, for trying to pull a fast one." Trey rolled his eyes and then sighed. Aubrey calmed everyone down, and Auston stayed on the floor; he sat back against the couch, as Aubrey spoke. "Alright, well now that y'all know what it is…just chill out when she's around, if she does come around us." They all nodded and then stood from their seats.

Trey looked at Aubrey. "I didn't fuck her again, because it was so bad, but it didn't stop her from wanting it again. I been going to work every night, but during the day, she's been hounding me. I knew something was wrong, since that wasn't like JoJo to do that, but I didn't think that this was happening again." Deon looked at his brother. "If she hounding you that bad, then take her to Max…drive her to Dallas." Mariya interjected. "No, she need to be here in Houston…Dallas is her territory, so she can't be there and slip away again. She was staying with Ricky, so he knows what needs to be done. Take her to his house."

They all thought that was a better idea. Trey nodded. "Yeah, I'ma do that, because I gotta work tonight, and I can't make that turn around trip." Aubrey nodded, and then everyone made their way out the apartment.

# Chapter 12

Aubrey's cellphone rang, as he was walking everyone out. Auston glanced at it on the end table and then slightly frowned, when he saw it was Kentay. Auston looked up and saw Aubrey occupied, so Auston quickly grabbed Aubrey's cell phone, and then yelled to Aubrey that he was going to the bathroom. Aubrey was laughing at something that Deon said, so didn't hear him.

Auston went to the bathroom and then answered the call, as he closed the door. "Hey…" Kentay smiled. "Hey, baby…I missed your call earlier, but I got your voicemail that it was urgent. So, what's going on?" Auston frowned, and then shook his head. Kentay frowned, while on the other end. "Baby, you there…?" Auston swallowed hard. "Uh huh…" Kentay slightly laughed. "Alright, what did I do? You're acting funny with me again…if this about last weekend, I told you that Auston was in town. Valentine's weekend is at the end of the week, so we can spend time together then. I told Auston that I had to work. It was supposed to be a damn surprise, but since you're mad now, then I hope you're not anymore." Kentay smiled, as Auston tried his best to control his anger.

Kentay was driving, so frowned, as he looked at his phone and then back to the road. "Baby, what's wrong? Talk to me…" Auston had enough. "Baby, huh? So, you and Aubrey been fucking around behind my damn back?" Kentay's eyes grew and he almost swerved off the road. "Auston?" Auston shook his head. "You sorry ass nigga…you and Aubrey been playin' me this whole damn time!" Auston flung the bathroom door open and almost ran into Aubrey. Aubrey frowned. "Auston, what's wrong?" Auston shook his head, and then put the phone on speaker; he held the phone up. "Which one of you niggas wanna start explaining this shit to me? Or lying to me?" Aubrey frowned and then heard Kentay. "Auston…I'm sorry, I'm really sorry." Aubrey looked at the phone and then to Auston. "Is that my phone?" Auston slowly nodded his head. "Yeah…but you can take your phone and the bitch nigga on the other line, with it." Auston tossed the phone to Aubrey, and he caught it.

Aubrey turned around and then quickly ran after Auston. "Auston, hold up…wait." He grabbed Auston's arm, and then Auston snatched it from Aubrey. "Don't fuckin' touch me…you're the one that introduced us!" Aubrey nodded. "I know, but it just started and…" Kentay interjected, since he was still on the phone. "It's my fault, Auston…I made the first move; he was messed up about Mike not taking him back and I wasn't thinking, but I started what we been doing. I'm sorry, Auston." Auston frowned, as he looked at the phone and then to Aubrey. "What the fuck? Mike don't want you, so you backtrack and take my damn dude? You took Mike from me and now Kentay…" Aubrey sighed and then looked away.

Auston shook his head, as Kentay had no more words to say. "I thought we agreed our friendship was more important, than fighting over any dude, but I see you didn't mean that shit. I don't mean shit to you either and probably never did. So, whatever you and Kentay are doing, y'all keep doing it…y'all got my damn blessing, because I don't want shit to do with neither one of y'all again." Aubrey looked back at Auston and then watched him walk away.

Aubrey sighed, after Auston slammed the door on his way out. Aubrey then looked back down at his cellphone. "He's gone, Kentay…" Kentay slightly nodded his head, as he drove. "Yeah, I got that, Aubrey…look, I'ma go…I'm on the road." Aubrey nodded. "Yeah, bye…" Aubrey ended the call and then shook his head, as he tossed his cellphone on the couch. Aubrey rubbed his hands down his face and then sighed. He walked to the kitchen to make himself a drink.

*　　*　　*

Later that evening, Ricky was on the couch and watching television, with others. The doorbell rang and Bullet got up to see who was at the door. He walked out the living room, and then Ricky went back to smoking, with Shooter.

Shortly after, Bullet returned to the living room. "Ricky…you need to come to the door." Ricky looked at Bullet and frowned. "For what?" Bullet cleared his throat. "You got somebody that wanna talk to you." Ricky looked at Shooter, and then put his blunt in the ashtray, before getting up from the couch. He walked past Bullet on his way out of the living room.

Ricky went to the front and then reached the door; he slightly frowned. "Do I know you?" Trey nodded. "Uh, I don't know…look, I'm JoJo's ex-husband, Trey…JoJo came to me last week and been staying with me." Ricky raised an eyebrow. "JoJo, huh?" Trey sucked his teeth. "Jaquelyn…I just found out what was going on today. I didn't know at first, but now that I know, it's best if she stays with you and you keep an eye on her. She's been tryin' to fuck since she got to my place…" Ricky frowned and then sighed; he nodded his head. "You gave in, didn't you?" Trey rolled his eyes. "Yeah, alright…I gave in once, and the shit was bad, so that's my fault. But now that I know it's not JoJo, it makes sense, and I want her out my damn apartment. My brother told all of us what was going on and the plan, so we're good on our end to keep the pretending going, but she needs to be with you, since it was your idea." Ricky nodded. "Yeah, she needs to be here…bring her in." Trey nodded and then turned around to go get Jovanni, since she was in the car.

Ricky turned back around and then returned to the living room. When he reached the living room, he stopped and then made an announcement. "Hey, y'all…JoJo's here…uh, Jaquelyn…y'all know the drill. She pretending to be JoJo, so keep the charade going." The guys nodded, and Shooter sighed.

Shortly after, Trey and Jovanni walked in the living room, and everyone looked at her. Trey cleared his throat and Ricky smiled. "Baby girl, come here…" Ricky walked over to her, and Jovanni met him in the middle; they hugged and then Ricky's smile faded, as he looked at Trey. "Uh, yeah…I'ma head out and go to work." Ricky nodded and then Jovanni let him go; she turned to Trey. "Hey, maybe I'll see you this weekend…it's my birthday and everybody is celebrating Valentine's Day, so maybe you can be my Valentine." Shooter frowned, as Ricky looked away. Trey slightly nodded his head. "Uh, yeah…JoJo. I don't know if I gotta work or not, but I'll see." Jovanni smiled and then nodded. "I wanna have a party, with everybody there, so you have to be there." Trey looked at Ricky and then back to her. "Yeah, sure…just let me know." She nodded and before he walked away, Jovanni grabbed his arm and then kissed him. Shooter put his hand over his face, as Ricky looked back at them and saw the display. Trey stopped the kiss and pulled back from Jovanni. "I gotta go, JoJo…" She nodded and then watched Trey walk out the living room.

After he left the house, Ricky addressed Jovanni. "You and Trey, huh? I thought that was over and done with." Jovanni shrugged her shoulders. "Me and Trey are just having a little fun, but I'm going back to Max when I'm ready…he can financially take care of me, but Trey can sexually take care of me." Shooter raised an eyebrow, as Ricky slightly nodded his head. "You ain't ask about your kids yet." Jovanni looked at Ricky. "I'm sure they're good…now where do I stay?" Ricky stared at her and then slightly nodded his head. "Shooter…show her to her room." Shooter nodded and then stood from the couch; he cleared his throat, as he walked out the living room, and Jovanni followed him with the one bag she had.

# Chapter 13

After they left, Ricky shook his head, as Bullet walked over to him. "What the fuck we gonna do with that here? Her personality can't be here that long, Ricky, or she gonna know what we into." Ricky looked at Bullet and then nodded. "Everything stops here, until this shit is straightened out with her...don't say nothing in front of her, don't do nothing, just don't... I'ma tell Shooter the same shit, when..." Before he could finish, they all heard yelling. Ricky frowned and then ran down the hall, as Bullet and another guy followed behind.

Once the guys reached the bedroom, they stopped, and Ricky continued to frown. "What the fuck?!" Jovanni quickly pushed Shooter off her, and then got up from the bed, as he did the same. Jovanni's shirt was pulled open, and she was in a panic. "He pulled my shirt open and then pushed me on the bed…he said he always wanted this with me. I tried to push him off." Shooter looked at Jovanni and then back to Ricky. "That shit ain't true! She's lyin'…! She did that shit to herself and then pulled me down on top of her!" Ricky clenched his jaw, and then slightly shook his head. "Get out the room, Shooter…" Shooter looked at Ricky and frowned. "What? Ricky, I ain't…" Ricky interjected. "Get out the fuckin' room, boy!" Shooter closed his mouth and then looked at Jovanni, before looking back at Ricky; he then stormed out the bedroom.

Ricky sighed, as he looked back at Jovanni. "You alright, baby girl?" She put her hand to her mouth and then shook her head. "I don't feel safe with him around." Ricky swallowed hard and then nodded. "Yeah, alright…" Jovanni nodded. "Can you make him leave…please daddy?" Ricky stared at her and then slightly nodded. "Uh, yeah…just uh, lay down and get settled. I'ma handle him." She nodded. "Thank you…"

Ricky grabbed the doorknob and then closed the door. Afterwards, he turned and saw his associates in his face. Bullet shook his head. "You know damn well Shooter wouldn't do that shit to JoJo." Ricky nodded. "Keep your voice down…" He jerked his head and then walked back down the hall, as everyone followed him.

Once back in the living room, Shooter stood from the couch. "Ricky, I ain't do what she said…you know I wouldn't do that shit to JoJo." Ricky nodded and then walked over to him. "I know…I know she's lyin', but you gotta go Shooter…just for a little while, until shit gets back right." Shooter frowned. "What the fuck you mean, I gotta go?" Ricky rubbed his hands down his face, and then looked back at Shooter. "She said she don't feel safe with you around, and if we're gonna keep this charade going, then I gotta make you leave…just for a little while. Jaquelyn don't know who you really are, and we're not gonna tell her, or she might suspect something."

Shooter looked at Bullet, who sighed and then walked over to the couch to sit down; the other guys did the same and walked away. Shooter looked back at Ricky. "I been living in this damn house most of my life and you kickin' me out now, because that bitch lied on me? Where the fuck I'ma go, Ricky?" Ricky took a deep breath. "I'm sorry…this how it gotta be until JoJo's mind comes back; Jaquelyn can't suspect shit." Shooter slightly nodded his head, and then swallowed hard. "I guess you gonna get rid of everybody when she do this to them too, huh? Or maybe you happy she picked me to do this to."

Ricky slightly shook his head, and then reached in pocket; he took some money out and tried to hand it to Shooter. "Take it…get a room or something." Shooter frowned, as he looked at the money and then back to Ricky. "That's what I'm worth, huh…a few dollars?" Ricky shook his head. "Boy, don't make this harder than it already is." Shooter made a sarcastic sound. "Yeah whatever, Ricky…" Shooter said nothing else, as he walked away from Ricky. Bullet put his hand over his face, as Ricky sighed. He turned to the guys. "Y'all stay away from JoJo from now on…if she come in here, y'all go somewhere else. I don't need her lyin' on nobody else around here, or she gonna make me kill her." Bullet stared at Ricky. "You was wrong, Ricky…Shooter been by your damn side longer than us; send that bitch somewhere else and let Shooter stay." Ricky sucked his teeth. "I can't…not right now. I'm going to my room…" Ricky walked out the living room, and Bullet sighed.

# Chapter 14

It was the weekend, and Ricky hadn't heard from Shooter since he left his house; he didn't show emotion publicly, but he did, privately and that night. Ricky missed his son and wanted him back home but knew that wasn't possible with Jovanni being there. Jovanni was insistent on having a birthday party and so wanted everyone there to enjoy her thirty-second birthday; a birthday that the real Jovanni would miss, since she was in jail.

*   *   *

Everyone was at the banquet hall, mostly everyone…Jovanni sent out announcements for her birthday party. Ricky had called Maxwell and informed him about the party, and he reluctantly said he would come to Houston. Jovanni wanted something grand for her birthday and wanted Trey by her side. Cyrus refused to be a part of this, and so stayed in Dallas with Bernadine; he agreed to watch Mickey and Mikey for the weekend, while Jax and Madison were at the house with Angeline and Allen watching them.

Deon walked over to Trey and then looked around, before looking back at him. "How you doing, man?" Trey looked at him and then shook his head. "She keeps calling me and shit…wanting me to come over. I swear I'm in a fuckin' nightmare." Deon shook his head and then Desiray walked over with Mariya. "Y'all look at this shit…JoJo wouldn't do no bullshit like this for her birthday." Mariya made a sarcastic sound. "Yeah, well last year she had something big, when she was with Stefan; he threw her that lavish birthday party that Jaquelyn got kicked out of." Deon laughed, as Desiray shook her head. Trey sucked his teeth. "How much longer we gotta keep this shit up, because for the first time in my life…JoJo is getting on my damn nerves?" Desiray frowned, as Mariya slightly laughed. "Ask Ricky, he's running this show, right?" Trey rolled his eyes and then Deon turned his head. "Uh, Ricky over there and throwing back shots, so maybe he's not in the mood to ask nothing to, right now."

Trey shook his head. "He's probably tired of her being at his damn house too." Before another word could be said, Jovanni walked over. "Hey guys…I'm about to make a speech in a little bit. I don't think any of you wanna miss it." She smiled and then walked away, as Deon gave a snide look and then rolled his eyes. "I'ma go get another drink." Trey sighed and then went with him. The women stood there and shook their heads.

As the party continued, Maxwell, Michael, and Stacee walked in the hall; Maxwell sighed. "Unbelievable…" Michael sighed. "Unbelievable is right…who the hell is paying for all this?" Maxwell glanced at his brother, as they walked to the bar. "Who the hell do you think? Ricky called me and said what "JoJo" wanted to do, so I had no choice but to foot the bill for this bullshit." Michael shook his head. "Wow…"

The guys reached the bar, and Maxwell quickly ordered a drink; Michael and Stacee did the same. Afterwards, Ricky walked down the bar and then asked for another drink. Maxwell looked at him. "How's it going, Ricky?" Ricky shot Maxwell a look, and Michael frowned with the angry look on his face. Ricky made a sarcastic sound. "How's it going? I'ma tell you how it's going…it's hell; that bitch accused Shooter of tryin' to rape her, the first fuckin' few minutes at my damn house. I had to tell him to leave…that's my damn son and I had to make him leave, when he been with me since he was a fuckin' kid. It's taking every damn thing I got not to kill that bitch." Stacee frowned, as Michael cleared his throat.

Maxwell looked at his brother and then back to Ricky. "Uh, I'm sorry, Ricky…" He shook his head and then grabbed his shot; he swallowed that down and then turned around to look out. Maxwell rubbed his hands down his face, and then grabbed his drink, after it was ready. Stacee leaned in to Michael. "Thanks for inviting me…out in public with you." Michael turned his head to him, after he grabbed his drink. "No problem…you're more than just a nanny." Michael sipped his drink, after he grabbed it from the bar counter. Stacee slightly nodded his head and then Auston walked over to the guys. Auston looked at Stacee, who he didn't know, and then to Michael. "Mike, can I talk to you?" Michael sighed and then nodded.

Michael excused himself from Stacee, and then walked a short distance with Auston. Once they were alone, Auston shook his head. "Did you know?" Michael frowned. "Did I know, what?" Auston sucked his teeth. "About Kentay and Aubrey…did you know?" Michael frowned. "Look, Auston…it's none of my business what goes on between Aubrey and anybody; we're not together and I moved on." Auston slightly nodded his head. "I don't believe that…Kentay's in Dallas with you, so…" Michael interjected. "So what, Auston? He's not in Dallas with me, he lives in Dallas. I just want you and Aubrey to leave me out of whatever is going on between you and him." Auston was about to say something, when Aubrey walked over, and Michael threw his hands up.

Aubrey looked between Michael and Auston. "What are y'all talking about?" Auston frowned and Michael rolled his eyes. "Not a damn thing…" Aubrey shot Michael a look. "Are y'all trying to hook back up?" Michael couldn't get a word out, before Auston started. "Are you fucking serious? What I do is none of your damn business or Kentay's…y'all can go fuck y'all selves." Aubrey sighed. "Auston, I said I was sorry…" Michael interjected. "Can I go now?" Aubrey looked at him. "No…" Michael frowned. "No? Look, this conversation has nothing to do with me, and I don't wanna hear anymore." Aubrey pushed Auston out the way and then looked at Michael again. "All you had to do was talk to me, but you blew me off for your damn nanny, some bitch nigga you just met. Kentay was there for me, and it just went from there." Michael and Auston both frowned, but for different reasons.

Auston grabbed Aubrey's shoulder, and then turned him around. "Why the fuck are you explaining that shit to him, when you fucked my dude?! You fucked Mike, when we were together!" Michael looked around when some started to look at them. Aubrey shook his head. "I said, I was sorry…it just happened. Kentay didn't even want you…he never got over me." Auston looked Aubrey up and down. "Oh, yeah? I'm sure all of a sudden, he didn't get over you, when you pulled your dick out for him." Aubrey sucked his teeth, and then Michael interjected. "Look, all of you can fight over one guy all you want, but I don't belong anywhere in this conversation, so I'm walking away." Michael turned around and almost ran into Stacee. "Hey, Mike…are you good?" Stacee eyed Aubrey and Auston, before looking back at Michael.

Michael cleared his throat and then nodded. "Yeah, I'm fine…let's go." Aubrey sighed. "Mike, I'm sorry…I went back to Kentay, because that's what I needed at the time. I still love you…and I'm fucking up left and right here, without you." Stacee frowned and didn't know what he walked into but was sure he needed to be a part of this conversation now. "Uh Aubrey, right? I don't know where you're going with this, but Mike don't want you. That's done and over with, so you need to move around in another direction." Auston laughed out loud, and then shook his head. Michael looked at Stacee and frowned, as Aubrey shot Stacee a look. "You don't know anything about this shit between me and Mike, so you need to walk your ass back wherever you came from. You're just the damn nanny, right?" Michael interjected. "I can speak for myself, and I already said to Aubrey, what I needed to say…what I wanted to be said, Stacee."

Stacee looked at Michael, and then saw how serious he was; he looked at Aubrey and then back to Michael. "Is that right? Well, I'ma just do what your man said and walk away…from both of y'all. I'm so fucking glad I know people in Houston…see you back in Dallas, Mike." Stacee said nothing else, as he walked away. Michael cursed to himself and then looked at Aubrey. Aubrey tried to touch Michael, but he snatched his arm away. "Don't touch me, Aubrey…I've had enough of this shit with you. You turned me down and I got over it, so you need to get over whatever mistake you feel you made, by turning me down to be together again."

Michael walked away and then Aubrey rubbed his hands down his face. He turned and saw Auston staring at him; he shook his head. "You messed over anything good you could of had with me, Kentay, or Mike, because you're selfish…you can't stand to see none of us with anybody else, if it's not with you. Maybe you'll keep fucking with Kentay, but he's probably the only one that don't love you and never did." Auston said nothing else, as he walked away. Aubrey sighed and then walked over to his brothers.

# Chapter 15

Michael went back over to Maxwell and saw that Stacee was gone; he left like he had said. Michael sighed and then asked for another drink. Shortly after, Jovanni got on the makeshift stage with the microphone; she tapped it and then got everyone's attention. Everyone looked at her, and Ricky rolled his eyes.

Jovanni had a smile on her face. "I just wanna thank everyone for coming…I'm having a great time with my friends and family…" She started to clap, and Deon frowned, as he and others clapped too. Jovanni continued. "Now…I share this day with someone else; she's not here right now…she's in jail. Jaquelyn is my twin sister and yes, she stabbed me, but it was in self-defense. She had a rough life…and I know she didn't mean to hurt me. I actually learned a lot from Jaquelyn;

she's really smarter than I thought…maybe even smarter than me." Maxwell frowned and then shot Michael a look. "What the fuck?" Michael sighed, as everyone else frowned too.

Jovanni continued. "Well…Jaquelyn is actually an inspiration, and I didn't give her enough credit…" Desiray rolled her eyes and Trey shook his head. Everyone was disgusted and wanted her to stop talking. Jovanni continued. "But my other inspiration is my twins…" Maxwell had the glass of alcohol to his mouth and then stopped short, when he heard her; he lowered his arm and prayed she didn't say a bad word about his twins.

Jovanni continued. "When I was pregnant, in jail…all I could think about was where my twins would be after they were born. I actually should be the one in jail, and Jaquelyn should be out…she didn't hurt me that bad. It was a small wound that I recovered from. I did kill a man…Stefan, but I'm free and I have a second chance to live my life…with Max…" She looked at him and then everyone turned their heads to him.

Maxwell looked around and then frowned, as Ricky stood by and clenched his jaw from the things that was said so far. Maxwell sighed and then Jovanni continued. "And this weekend…I'm going home with my man, Max, and be with our twins." Maxwell frowned. "What?!" Michael looked at him and then nudged him in the side. Maxwell looked at his brother and then back to Jovanni. Trey looked at Maxwell and knew he didn't want Jaquelyn's personality around his twins, so he decided to help him out. "Hold on,

JoJo…I thought you wanted me back?" Deon shot his brother a look and frowned, as Maxwell and others looked at him.

Trey ran to the podium and then grabbed the microphone from her. "Uh, Max…I'm sorry, but I…I fucked JoJo the other night." Jovanni frowned and Aubrey's jaw dropped. Michael had his mouth open, and Ricky shook his head. Maxwell made a few steps. "You did what? You fucked her?!" Trey swallowed hard and then nodded his head, as Jovanni grabbed the microphone from him; she then looked at Maxwell. "Uh Max, I can explain…I came home and just…well, I needed that, and Trey gave it to me, but it didn't mean anything." Maxwell looked at his brother, who was in disbelief. Ricky walked over to Maxwell and then grabbed his arm to turn him around. "Keep your cool…that dude tryin' to save you up there, so she won't be around your kids." Maxwell slightly nodded his head, and then turned his head back to Jovanni. "You fucked another man, and you think I want you after that? You're not coming home to me…JoJo, so stay in Houston with him." Maxwell swallowed hard, as Michael shook his head.

Jovanni slightly nodded her head and then cleared her throat. "Fine…it's alright. Twins share men all the time, so if not you, then Jaquelyn's old flame, Preston…or maybe just me and Trey; we were talking about getting back together anyway…" Trey frowned, as Maxwell shook his head. Desiray and Mariya looked at each other while in disbelief. Jovanni thanked everyone and then grabbed Trey's hand, before she pulled him off the makeshift stage.

Maxwell turned to his brother. "I don't know how much more of this I can take. She's using my woman's body and turning her into a fucking whore." Michael looked around and then back to his brother. "Keep your voice down..." Ricky interjected, and the guys looked at him. "He's right...you talkin' too damn loud...there ain't a damn thing we can do, until JoJo's mind comes back to where it belongs. So, just keep letting Jaquelyn run her damn mouth." Maxwell shook his head. "She's doing more than running her damn mouth...she's opening her legs for any and everybody. She's doing this shit on purpose, Ricky. She knows damn well, JoJo wouldn't act like this. It's like she's mocking JoJo and who she was. Did you hear that shit she said up there...praising Jaquelyn, herself? Please...JoJo hated Jaquelyn; she'd never say that... and now I have to deal with her and Trey. My body, fucking Trey!" Michael put his hand over his face, as Ricky looked around and then back to Maxwell. "Max, shut up...you not the only one suffering from this bullshit; she fuckin' up everybody's damn life right now, so hold on." Maxwell shook his head. "I went to see JoJo in jail...she was in a damn fight in there with some dike with tear drop tattoos under her eye. Either she's gonna kill somebody in there and get new charges against her...or get killed by somebody." Ricky sighed and then rubbed his hand down his face; he hadn't returned to Dallas to see her in jail, so wasn't aware of this.

Michael sighed. "Please, stop thinking about this, Max...before you make yourself sick. You don't have a choice but to wait for this to play out." Maxwell took a deep breath and then nodded. Shortly after, Trey walked over and then looked between the men. "Hey…we got a big ass problem." Ricky and the guys looked at Trey, as he shook his head. "She said she's pregnant…" Ricky slapped his forehead with his hand and then turned around. Maxwell didn't think he heard what he did. "Excuse me? She's pregnant?" Michael cleared his throat and then turned around at the bar to ask for another drink. Trey sighed and then nodded. "Yeah…but if she is, then it's not mine; we used a condom…and it didn't last long enough for me to nut no way, so I know I wouldn't be the daddy." Michael frowned, after he turned around. "What?"

Trey sighed. "It's JoJo's body, but she fucks like Jaquelyn, which don't say much, since she's the most inexperienced grown woman I ever met." Ricky frowned, after he turned back to Trey. Maxwell swallowed hard, and then put his hand up. "How far along, Trey?" Trey sighed. "I don't know…but the crazy thing is, she took it back and then said she wanted a baby. I told her that wasn't happening with me, so she didn't say nothing else and just walked away. I don't know what's true or not since she's nothing but a liar." The guys frowned, as Maxwell felt he couldn't breathe. Ricky frowned and then slightly shook his head. "Was Jaquelyn tested at the jail or in the hospital after her accident?" Maxwell looked at him and then shrugged his shoulders. "I don't know…" Michael believed he knew where Ricky was going with this. "The Jaquelyn sitting in jail might be pregnant or she could care less about the twins you have and wants a baby by somebody else, to raise."

Maxwell shot his brother a look. "I can't take this anymore…so if she really wants a baby then she can just go out and fuck some random guy to get knocked up by." Trey shook his head. "Not random…Preston Worthing." Maxwell almost passed out, and Michael and Ricky had to grab Maxwell, to hold him up. They moved him back to sit down on a bar stool. He started to sweat, and Michael asked for a wet towel. Trey sighed, as Michael grabbed the towel and then used it on his brother's forehead. "Max, calm down…does Preston know what's going on? Does he know who she really is?" Maxwell looked at Michael. "It won't matter…Preston won't believe something like this." Ricky interjected. "You said Preston? Bellfort Randy the one that told me that Jaquelyn came to her first, before her accident; she said she was with Preston, but Jaquelyn left him, 'cause she knew he'd be pissed having her there if she was a wanted woman…so if he know what Jaquelyn did now, he won't let her come back in his life, but JoJo…this JoJo, he's not gonna turn her down." Maxwell didn't find that comforting and now wanted to leave.

Music started to play and then the guys turned their heads. Jovanni was dancing and Trey frowned. "Oh my God…" Michael raised an eyebrow. "I don't understand how Jaquelyn could possibly think nobody would know she wasn't JoJo…I've seen JoJo dance before and no offense Max, but it's enough to get a guy's dick hard." They all looked at Michael and he cleared his throat. "Anyways, I'm ready to go; you, Max?" Maxwell gave his brother a snide look and then rolled his eyes. "Yes…maybe I can erase this entire night out of my head." Maxwell stood from the stool, as Michael put the towel on the bar counter. "Ricky, we're heading back to the hotel, and then going back to Dallas tomorrow. You should go see JoJo…." Ricky nodded and then Trey said he was going back to his friends. After he walked away, Ricky looked at the guys. "I'ma stay a little longer and see where her head's at. If she tryin' to leave Houston or not. Whatever she do, I'ma call." Maxwell nodded and then he and Michael walked out the hall. Ricky sighed, as he sat down on the bar stool and then asked for another drink; he turned around on the stool and looked out, as some of the partygoers started to loosen up after consuming alcohol.

# Chapter 16

The party had died down and many were grateful that it was over. Ricky stayed there the entire time, even though he didn't want to. Jovanni's friends left as soon as they could and didn't bother telling her goodbye. Ricky was the last one standing and then told Jovanni that he was taking her home, just to make sure that she went home and nowhere else. Jovanni was drunk about time she left the hall and Ricky had to practically carry her out to his car.

Afterwards, they went back to his house; he put her in the bed and then left the bedroom. For the rest of the weekend, many of the gang weren't in the mood to celebrate Valentine's, so didn't. Maxwell and Michael returned to Dallas and without Stacee. Michael tried to call Stacee, but his calls and text messages were ignored.

Everyone saw Jovanni in action, with Jaquelyn's personality and were taken aback by how she was acting. Ricky had it in the back of his head that it was possible, Jovanni would never return to her normal self.

It was the following week and Valentine's Day had come and gone; Desiray and Deon went out together, after he got off work; Aubrey spent it alone, as well as Auston and Kentay. Mariya had a date, Cyrus and Bernadine spent their evening at home, while Nathan and Bella got together. Michael and Maxwell spent the day alone.

*     *     *

Michael was home from work and had the boys with him; he had to ask Maxwell if his staff could watch the boys for him, for the past few days, since Stacee was still gone.

Michael entered the house with both baby carriers and their diaper bags on his shoulders. He sighed, as he closed the door with his foot, and then made his way to the living room. He set the baby carriers down and then the diaper bags. Michael sat down on the couch and then took a deep breath; he shook his head and then started to unstrap both boys. As he did this, he heard the front door and then slightly turned his head. He then got back to the boys.

Stacee entered the living room with his keys in his hand; he saw what Michael was doing, so tossed his keys on the couch. Michael looked behind him and then back to Stacee; he saw that his eyes were bloodshot red.

Michael stood from the couch with a frown on his face. "Are you serious? You come in my house, days later with no phone call or text message, and apparently drunk and high." Stacee waved his hand around. "What the fuck do you care...? I'm back, so chill out." Stacee walked over to the boys and then smiled. "Hey...hey Mikey, hey Mickey..." Michael pushed Stacee back. "Get away from them...and don't come near them again, until you sober the fuck up." Stacee frowned, and then Michael continued. "Where've you been and who were you with?" Stacee sucked his teeth. "Why? Like you care who I was laid up with these past few days..." Michael frowned and then slowly nodded his head. "So, you were laid up with who? Another man, or woman?" Stacee waved his hand around. "You're asking too many questions...just know that I was happy and fucking the whole time I was in Houston."

Stacee tried to walk away, and Michael angrily grabbed his arm. Stacee looked at his arm and then back to Michael. "Let me go..." Stacee snatched his arm from Michael, and then made a sarcastic sound. "I knew I should of stayed in Houston...I got treated much better there, than I do here. Did I mention I used to live in Houston and worked the babysitting scene there too? A lot of horny women with kids, that wanna be taken care of...you call me nanny, they call me daddy." Stacee laughed and then shook his head, as he walked away from Michael; he yawned and then made his way to his bedroom. Michael sighed and then went back to the boys.

After some time, Michael had fed the boys, given them a bath, and then put them to bed; it had taken him awhile to accomplish this, since he was used to

Stacee doing it or helping him.

It was close to eleven at night about time that Michael finished. He was tired and went to take a shower, after he put the boys to bed; it was a quick shower and then afterwards, he went to the nursery to check on the boys, before going downstairs and finding himself something to eat. Michael hadn't eaten anything in two days and was literally running on fumes, since he had to work and take care of the boys by himself.

Michael walked into the kitchen and then stopped when he saw Stacee; he sighed and then walked over to the refrigerator, as Stacee glanced at him. "What are you doing?" Michael spoke, while looking in the refrigerator. "None of your damn business…" Stacee was eating a bowl of cereal, and then slightly nodded his head. "Alright…but I can make you something if you want." Michael stopped what he was doing and then slammed the refrigerator door, before he turned around. "Are you fucking bipolar or something? Did you forget already that you strolled in my damn house, after a few days, while drunk and high?" Stacee chewed his cereal, as he listened to Michael; he then shook his head. "Nope, I didn't forget…but I'm good now. I popped some pills and slept it off…" Michael sighed. "Well good for you…I'm going to bed."

Michael was about to walk out the kitchen, when his stomach growled and very loudly. Stacee sighed. "I know you're hungry…so let me make you something to eat, before we go to bed." Michael turned around and frowned. "Excuse me? We? I think you might still be drunk and high, if you think 'we' are going to bed together." Stacee continued to chew his cereal, as if he didn't have a care in the world. "I think you must be drunk and high, if you think I'ma let you talk to me any kind of way…and especially in front of your reject exes." Michael raised an eyebrow, as he stared at Stacee, who hadn't looked up from his bowl of cereal yet.

Michael slightly nodded his head. "My exes are my business, and you shouldn't of came over and said a word to either of them, because I didn't need back-up for a damn thing." Stacee put another spoonful of cereal in his mouth, before he spoke. "You brought me to that party, so I don't appreciate you walking away from me to go talk to either of your exes. If you didn't want me there, then you shouldn't of invited me." Michael frowned; he turned his head to the side and then back to Stacee. "I'm tired of you being jealous over men I don't even want anymore…so if you can't control your temper or get your jealousy in check, then you need to leave." Stacee finally looked up at Michael and had a blank look on his face, as he finished chewing his cereal. "Are you done?" Michael raised an eyebrow. "What?"

Stacee stood from the stool, and then went to the sink to wash the bowl and spoon; he spoke while at the sink. "Mike, I know you like to be in control…I saw that the first time I walked in your damn house; you gotta to be in control or you can't function. So, I made a scenario that you had no control of…I took off and partied in Houston, then I came back when I felt like it. You had no control over that…because you got no control over me, and you can't stand that."

Stacee finished at the sink, and then dried the bowl and spoon, before he put them up; he turned around and then leaned against the sink, as he stared at Michael. "Yeah, I got drunk and high…there's not a damn thing you can do about that. I know you had it rough doing everything by yourself for a few days, but once again…you had no control over that, and had to do it, because I was gone." Michael continued to stare at Stacee, as he continued. "I already know that you thought about me the whole time I was gone…wondering what I was doing and who I was doing. You act like you don't care, but I know you do." Michael slightly nodded his head. "So, you did this on purpose?" Stacee slightly smiled. "Did you miss me?" Michael turned his head to the side and then back to Stacee. "I don't like games…I've played them before and it got me nowhere, so if you're trying to play games with me now, then I don't care what you think or say, you're out of here." Stacee slightly nodded his head. "Alright, cool…and since this nanny wasn't missed, then I'ma go back to Houston on my weekends off."

Stacee pushed himself from the counter and then made his way out the kitchen. Michael put his arm out to stop him. Stacee looked at Michael. "Are you gonna move out my way, Mike?" Michael didn't look at Stacee but stayed staring out straight. "I'm sorry…and I did miss you. If you want a label, then you don't get paid anymore. So, what's more important…the money or me?" Stacee stared at him. "You actually thought I cared about the money more than you? I love you, Mike, but you're pissing me off…Aubrey is pissing me off too, so if I hear that dude say I'm just a nanny, one more time, then that's on you, for not correcting him or anybody else." Michael finally turned his head to Stacee and then sighed. Before he could say a word, Stacee did again. "Now that we cleared all that up…are 'we' going to bed, or do I need to make my man something to eat?" Michael stared at Stacee and then slightly shook his head. "I'm not hungry anymore…" Stacee nodded. "Alright…" Michael leaned in and then kissed Stacee; after a few moments, they stopped, and Michael pulled back from him. "I love you too…" Stacee slightly smiled. "I know…I just been waiting for you to say it. Come on…let's go to bed." Michael nodded and then Stacee took his hand; he pulled Michael out the kitchen and then they went upstairs, to go to bed.

# Chapter 17

One month later…

Jaquelyn walked out, while handcuffed, and to the bench where Maxwell was waiting for her; he cringed at how she looked. Maxwell swallowed hard and then shook his head, as Jaquelyn sat down. Maxwell sighed. "Baby, what happened to you?" She sighed and then shook her head. "I wish I wasn't liked so damn much. I keep fighting this same dike up in here that's been trying to fuck me, since I got here. These war wounds are apparently turning her on even more, since she's got the same ones." Maxwell sighed and then slightly shook his head. "What can I do?" Jaquelyn made a sarcastic sound. "Not a damn thing…I wish you'd stop coming here, Max. Every time I gotta watch you walk away…" Jaquelyn stopped and then sighed, as Maxwell nodded. "I know and I'm sorry…but I can't help it. I have to see you, baby…every time I look at Madison, I see you…she looks just like her mama, and I tell her that every damn day. I show them your picture, so they won't forget you."

Jaquelyn slightly nodded her head, and then quickly wiped her eyes, as she sighed. "Yeah…uh, Ricky came to see me." Maxwell sighed and knew she wanted the subject to change, so he would comply with what she wanted. "That's good…the last time I saw him was at JoJo's, uh, Jaquelyn's birthday party, that I had to pay for. It's been rough on everybody dealing with her; she's taking on your life, like it's her own." Jaquelyn nodded. "I bet she is…but uh, I guess there's nothing that can be done about that now." Maxwell shook his head. "Baby, come on, we…" Jaquelyn interjected. "No…we're both awake and not in a damn coma. I don't know how this works or why this is happening, but I'm going away for at least thirty years."

Maxwell's eyes became watery, and then he shook his head. "JoJo…she's being reckless; she's in Dallas and with Preston. I'm thinking he should know what happened by now, with Jaquelyn stabbing you, and wants nothing to do with her, but more than willing to be with her twin sister, JoJo…" Jaquelyn frowned and then shook her head, as she rose up straight.

Jaquelyn put her hand to her mouth and then dropped it; she stared at Maxwell, as he slightly looked down. Jaquelyn slightly leaned her head to the side, as she stared at him. "What else are you not telling me?" Maxwell looked back at her. "Uh, she's trying to get pregnant…or maybe she already is, I don't know, and I don't wanna know. I can't know something like that, because if she is, then that means when you two switch back, then…" Jaquelyn interjected. "Then I'ma be pregnant or already have a baby by Preston Worthing…" Maxwell nodded his head and Jaquelyn shook hers. "Well, how come you didn't get back with her? She didn't want you?" Maxwell sighed. "She did, but I don't want her around Madison and Jax…she's not their mama." Jaquelyn nodded. "She is their mama…" Maxwell rolled his eyes. "You know what I mean, JoJo…I didn't want her to hurt one of them or do something to them." Jaquelyn sucked her teeth. "So, you want me pregnant with Preston's baby? Because that's what's gonna happen…if she wants a fucking baby, then you get her pregnant. At least it'll still be ours."

Maxwell stared at her and then turned his head to the side. Jaquelyn told him to look at her, and then he turned his head back to her. "Max…I can't do anything from here. I didn't want any more kids, but if I gotta have another one, then I damn sure don't want one by Preston Worthing. It's still my body…it's still my body, so please…do something." Maxwell wiped his eyes and then slightly nodded his head. "Yeah, alright…I'll try to talk to her or something." Jaquelyn nodded and then sighed. "Don't come back here again…" Maxwell frowned and tried to protest this, but she put her hand up to stop him. "Don't, Max…just don't come back." Maxwell sighed and then nodded; he stood from the bench and before he walked away, she stopped him. Maxwell looked at her, as she stood from the bench too. "Talk to Preston…and tell my sister…JoJo, that I wanna see her; make her come see me." Maxwell slightly nodded. "So, you don't want me to talk to her?" Jaquelyn shook her head. "No…I think I got an idea:

just trust me. Talk to Preston…only." Maxwell nodded and then told her goodbye; she watched him walk away and then she sighed. If Jovanni was going to get her life and body back, then she had to think outside the box, and get her hands a little dirty.

# Chapter 18

It was later in the day and Jaquelyn was sitting at a table, while not eating, like everyone else was. She sighed and then pushed her tray away from her. As she sat there, the woman that Jaquelyn had been fighting since she got in jail, had walked over to her with other women.

Jaquelyn turned her head, and then rolled her eyes; she sighed, as the woman put her leg up on the spot next to Jaquelyn. "You like what you see…big tits?" Jaquelyn sighed and then shook her head, as she stared at the woman, who everyone called 'Timber'. "Really? Hell no, I don't like what I see…how many fucking times we gotta do this, Timber, I mean really?" Timber frowned and then removed her leg; she cracked her knuckles, and then Jaquelyn decided to enact her plan.

"Hey, Timber…let me talk to you, alone…" She looked at the women with Timber, and then back to her. Timber looked at the women and then jerked her head; they walked away and then Timber sat down, next to Jaquelyn. "So, now you wanna talk instead of fight? You gonna give me some pussy?" Jaquelyn frowned and then waved her hand around. "No, look…I got a twin sister; she framed me, and her ass is supposed to be in here, not me. I need your help, and you're the roughest person in here that I can ask." Timber frowned and stared at Jaquelyn as if she was crazy. "Bitch, I ain't your friend." Jaquelyn made a sarcastic sound. "You're right about that, but anyway, my twin sister…if she's in here, then you can do whatever you want with her; she can't fight worth a damn, so that's easy prey for you. I don't give a fuck about her, so I'm giving you my word, that when she gets in here…you can have that bitch."

Timber listened to Jaquelyn and then looked around, before looking back at her. "This legit…?" Jaquelyn nodded. "Yeah…so can I trust you to keep your mouth shut, because I know you got one more time to fuck up before they up your charges?" Timber frowned. "How you know all that?" Jaquelyn slightly smiled. "There's a lot of women in here that don't like you…they like me; in reality the number of women that hate you, outnumber you and your little crew that you walk around with. So, I'll make sure they don't slit your throat in your sleep, if you help me out." Timber sucked her teeth and then shook her head. "You lyin', big tits…" Jaquelyn continued to stare at Timber. "You wanna test your theory or mine?"

Timber looked around and saw a few stares coming her way; she looked in another direction and saw the same thing. Timber looked back at Jaquelyn and then sighed. "Alright…what you need help with?" Jaquelyn grinned. "Ok, well I need to know if you're cool with any of the guards and maybe somebody in the infirmary?" Timber looked around and then back to Jaquelyn. "Why? What you tryin' to do, escape?" Jaquelyn sighed and then shook her head. "In a way, yeah…but not how you think. My sister put me in here for something she did, so I want her ass in here…if you help me, then I got you when you get out. I can get you a job…it won't be legit, but you're gonna make money." Timber slightly nodded her head. "What exactly you tryin' to do, big tits?" Jaquelyn rolled her eyes at the nickname that Timber gave her; she then sighed. "I need to be unconscious, and I need her to be unconscious too, at the same time." Timber frowned. "What the fuck? You for real?" Jaquelyn nodded.

Timber shook her head. "Her, knocked the fuck out, I get. But you too…why?" Jaquelyn shook her head. "It's a long ass story and you wouldn't believe me if I told you anyway. I'm not crazy, but the infirmary part…she's allergic to a type of anesthesia, and I'm not…so if I can get my hands on that anesthesia, I can do damage to her." Timber sighed. "And what you gonna do to yourself?" Jaquelyn sighed and then rubbed her hands down her face. "We gotta get this right, no fuck-ups…so just slam my head into the wall." Timber frowned, and then slightly laughed. "Damn, bitch…you fuckin' crazy. You for real about this shit too, huh?" Jaquelyn nodded and then Timber sucked her teeth. "Alright, look…I got a few connections in here, and good with one of the guards; he a shady nigga, so I know he won't give a fuck. I can get what you need too, so I'ma help you." Jaquelyn nodded and then Timber eyed her. Jaquelyn rolled her eyes. "No, Timber…" Timber sucked her teeth. "Yeah, alright…" Timber got up, and then walked away from Jaquelyn. Jaquelyn watched her leave and then sighed; she prayed that this worked, because if it didn't, Jovanni could lose her body and possibly her life, for good.

# Chapter 19

Michael was at the house and in the kitchen; he was cutting fruit, when Stacee walked in the kitchen with a smile on his face. Michael glanced at him, and then looked back down at what he was doing. "What has you so happy today?" Stacee frowned and then walked over to Michael; he stood behind him and then kissed him on the neck. "I got a job today…" Michael stopped cutting the fruit. Stacee moved from behind Michael, and then grabbed a piece of cantaloupe from the cutting board. Michael looked at him. "A job? What job and for what?" Stacee frowned, as he looked at Michael and chewed. "A congratulations would of been nice, first…but don't worry I got a night gig, so I can still be here for the boys when you go to work." Michael slightly frowned. "A night job, where?" Stacee slightly cleared his throat. "Don't trip, Mike…I got another babysitting job, but hear me out…" Michael dropped the knife, and then walked around the kitchen island to leave the kitchen. "I don't wanna hear it, Stacee." Stacee turned around and followed Michael out the kitchen. "Mike, wait…just listen to me."

Michael stopped in the living room, and then turned around to Stacee. "Listen to what? So, now you're going back to fucking horny housewives again?" Stacee shook his head. "No, I'ma actually be watching kids, while their mama works at night. Sixteen an hour, from ten to six in the morning, so I'll be back home before you leave, and I can still put the boys down for the night, before I go." Michael stared at Stacee, as if he lost his mind. Stacee sighed. "Baby, I need a job…I need to make money." Michael slightly nodded his head. "Money, huh?" Stacee rolled his eyes. "I'm not your nanny anymore, Mike. I'm your man now, so…" Stacee slightly frowned, when Michael turned his head to the side. Stacee stepped a little closer to Michael. "You still think of me as your nanny, don't you?" Michael looked back at Stacee and then sighed. "I don't call you that anymore, Stacee." Stacee stared at Michael and then nodded. "I know you don't, but I guess that's not stopping you from still thinking it. So, I guess you still see me as the help, but somebody you don't have to pay anymore." Michael shook his head. "You wanted the title of my man, and you have it…but it doesn't stop me from thinking of you as something else too." Stacee frowned. "I'm not your fucking nanny anymore, Mike. I take care of the boys with you, as your damn man, not their nanny. How about you just hire somebody else and make this easy?"

Michael sighed and then nodded. "Ok, fine…you're not my nanny anymore, so I'm just gonna hire somebody to work at night, when you're gone." Stacee nodded. "Thank you…" Michael shook his head and then stepped closer to Stacee; he kissed him and then pulled back from him. "Go take your nap and while the boys are asleep, I'll find a new nanny." Stacee nodded, and then turned around to walk out the living room; he went upstairs and then Michael sighed. Michael walked out the living room, and then went to his office to find a nanny on his computer.

*   *   *

It was the following week, and Jovanni was led to an interrogation type room, and not the regular visiting area. It took the rest of the previous week and a couple days of this week, for Jaquelyn to tweak her plan and get help from others. Maxwell was able to convince Jovanni to go see Jaquelyn in jail.

Jaquelyn sat there and then waited; the door opened, and a guard walked in with Jovanni behind him. Jaquelyn looked at him and he looked at her, before walking out and closing the door. Jovanni sat down in the chair and then slightly smiled. "Jaquelyn…it's good to see you." Jaquelyn stared at her and then slightly nodded her head. "Fuck you, Jaquelyn…you know damn well you're not me and could never be me, but I heard you been really showing out. You really think nobody could tell the difference between us?" The real Jaquelyn grinned and then shrugged her shoulders. "Well, Max couldn't tell us apart, so why would anybody else? I mean, I was confused when I woke up in that hospital…they kept calling me your name, and after they kept explaining to me what was going on, it finally clicked in my head, that this was real. That I was in your body and…you had to be in mine."

The real Jovanni slightly shook her head. "Yeah, well…all good things must come to an end, Jaquelyn…" The real Jaquelyn laughed and then shook her head. "You're delusional, JoJo…I mean, I'm having so much fun being you. I practically get away with anything and get what I want from anyone. I fucked Trey…I fucked Preston…I fucked this random guy I met…I tried to fuck Shooter, but he wasn't acting right, so I had to tell Ricky that he tried to rape me; Ricky kicked him to the curb." The real Jovanni frowned and then clenched her jaw. "You lied on Shooter? You fucking bitch…" She stood from the chair with anger on her face, and then looked at the clock on the wall, before looking back at her sister. "I'm happy you had so much fun, fucking up everybody's life, but you're gonna give me back my damn body…or we're both gonna die, if this don't work." The real Jaquelyn frowned. "What?"

Before another word could be said, loud alarms started to go off; the real Jovanni ran around the table and then punched the real Jaquelyn in the face. Jaquelyn fell out the chair and onto the floor. Jovanni kicked her in the stomach twice, and then grabbed Jaquelyn by the hair, to pick her up from the floor. She looked at her. "I'd rather die than let you keep living in my damn body, you bitch!" Jovanni slammed Jaquelyn's face, in reality, her face, into the table multiple times. Shortly after, the door opened, and then Timber and the guard that made eye contact, ran in. Jovanni flung

Jaquelyn to the floor and then looked at Timber. "Y'all got it?" Timber nodded, as she looked at her and then to Jaquelyn on the floor. "Damn, you wasn't lyin'…you really JoJo?" Jovanni nodded and the guard frowned. "Y'all hurry the fuck up…three minutes, JoJo." She nodded, and then he grabbed the syringe from his pocket; he then gave it to Jovanni.

Jovanni bent over Jaquelyn, as she moaned and groaned; she injected Jaquelyn with something and then pulled it back out her arm. Jovanni rose back up and then handed the syringe back to the guard; he looked at his watch. "Come on, JoJo…" Jovanni nodded and then she and Timber hugged. "Hopefully, I'll see you on the other side…" She pulled back from Timber. "Remember what I told you…if this works." Timber nodded, and the guard yelled. "One minute!" Jovanni took a deep breath. "Do it!" Timber grabbed Jovanni, swung her around, and then slammed her head into the wall. Jovanni bounced off the wall, and then fell to the floor; she and Jaquelyn were now unconscious on the floor.

Timber reached down and then grabbed all the items in Jaquelyn's purse; she then handed them to the guard, as he stared at Jovanni. He shook his head. "Oh, shit…let's go…let's go…come on!" The guard opened the door, and then he and Timber ran out.

# Chapter 20

It was early the next morning, around five, when Stacee got home from his night job; he walked in the house, and then turned the silent alarm off. Stacee hung his keys on the wall, and then closed the door, before he rubbed his hands down his face. Stacee walked to the kitchen to grab a bottle of water; when he reached the kitchen, he stopped and then frowned, when he saw a shirtless, unidentified man, pouring juice at the kitchen island. "What the fuck?" The guy looked up and then raised an eyebrow. "Uh, do you work here too?" Stacee continued to frown, as he stared at the unknown guy. "What the fuck do you mean, do I work here too? I live here? Who the hell are you?" The guy set the juice container down on the counter. "I'm Kevin…the nanny. I never seen you before, so are you sure you live here?" Stacee was outdone, and then turned around to run out the kitchen. He ran to the stairs and then took them, two at a time. After he reached the top, he stormed into Michael's bedroom, since the door was open. Stacee flipped the switch to turn the lights on. Michael shifted in the bed, and then rolled over; he opened his eyes and then saw Stacee. "What time is it?" Stacee frowned. "Who the fuck cares what time it is? Who's that dude downstairs with no damn clothes on?"

Michael rose in the bed, and then rubbed his hands down his face to wake up; he looked at the clock on the nightstand and then back to Stacee. "You're home early, why?" Stacee raised an eyebrow, as he stared at Michael. "You got another guy in the house at night, when I'm gone, and you're asking me why I'm home early? Why is he here and saying he's the nanny?" Michael sighed. "Because he is the nanny…you told me to hire somebody else to work here at night, when you're gone, so I did. He's been here since last week…he's always gone before you get home, I guess until this morning."

Stacee shook his head, as he walked over to the bed. "Are you a straight up lunatic, Mike? Who does that shit? I thought you were gonna hire a woman, not a man." Michael shrugged his shoulders. "What difference does it make? Besides, I found him the same way I found you…word of mouth; apparently there's a lot of guys like you out there, but he does his business during the day and not at night." Stacee frowned and then made a sarcastic sound. "Are you trying to piss me off, Mike? He's been here since last week and you didn't even tell me? What if I came home early another night and found him here? I could of shot him or something."

Michael yawned, as he flung the covers off him and then got out of bed. Stacee's jaw dropped. "What the fuck? You really went to bed naked, with that guy walking around the house?" Michael glanced at Stacee and then walked to the dresser; he yawned again, as he grabbed some underwear and then put them on. "Stacee, it's too damn early for all this…it's the weekend and I wanted to sleep in. Since you said you wanted your weekends, then Kevin will be here for me, on the weekends."

Michael walked past Stacee, and then out the bedroom. Stacee turned around and then followed him to the boys' nursery. Michael checked on the boys and saw that they were still asleep; he then walked out with Stacee still behind him. Michael made his way downstairs and then to the kitchen, where Kevin still was. Michael walked in the kitchen and Kevin looked at him. "Good morning, Mr. Marshall…" He looked at Stacee. "Does he work here?" Michael looked at Stacee and then back to Kevin; he shook his head. "Not anymore…" Kevin slowly nodded his head. "You want me to get rid of him?" Stacee frowned, as he looked at Kevin. "You touch me, and I break your arm…you touch him, and I break your arm; either way, you're gonna get your arm broken." Michael frowned, as he looked at Stacee; he sighed and looked back at Kevin. "I'm up, if you wanna go ahead and go…" Kevin glanced at Stacee, and then looked at Michael. "I'm staying for the rest of the weekend; you said you wanted me." Stacee raised an eyebrow and then sarcastically laughed. "Look here, Kevin…Mike don't want you, so don't ever get confused about that, while you're here." Michael rolled his eyes. "Uh, Kevin…just leave us alone for a minute…go ahead and go to your bedroom and check on the boys while you're up there." Kevin nodded, as Stacee frowned. "While he's up there? His fucking bedroom is upstairs with you?"

Michael turned to Stacee and then shook his head. "I don't see you anymore…I'm at work during the day, when you're here, then when I get home, you're usually asleep. You wake up and if the boys are asleep, then you leave the house. Kevin comes and then takes over. Last weekend I spent it with him…and you didn't even notice that somebody else was here. You just happened to leave work early this morning and came home, otherwise you wouldn't of saw him."

Stacee sighed. "Mike, did you ever live with somebody before? A roommate, your brother, anybody that meant something to you?" Michael sighed and then shook his head. "No…" Stacee slightly nodded. "Well, I have…it's annoying to have a roommate, no privacy when you live with your parents, and fucking irritating to live with a girlfriend. If this is your first time living with somebody then you can't do what you did; you can't have another man or woman at the house at night, when your damn man is at work. I know you wouldn't want me having somebody here in the house while you're at work…and at night is worse, than during the day. You sleep naked and apparently that guy will do anything for you, Mr. Marshall." Michael slightly laughed, as Stacee rolled his eyes. "I hate you, Mike…you're fucking killing me." Michael sighed and then rubbed his hands down his face. "Stacee, you don't have to work if you don't want to…I'm not forcing you to work. You can go back to doing what you were doing, and I can go back to paying you, if you want. Whatever I have to do so you won't be gone at night, and at home in the damn bed."

Stacee sighed and then nodded. "Maybe I can just find another job…because I'm not gonna let you pay me. And as much as you don't want me gone at night, I don't want that guy here with you at night." Michael nodded. "Alright, well Kevin stays on the night shift until you find a day job…then he goes to days…deal?" Stacee sucked his teeth; as much as he wanted to say no, he didn't and agreed. Michael nodded and then kissed Stacee. Afterwards, he told Stacee to take a shower and then lay down. Stacee nodded and then walked out the kitchen; Michael watched him and then sighed.

# Chapter 21

Later in the day, Ricky had just arrived home with Bullet; he had been trying to call Shooter since the previous month, but Shooter ignored all his calls. Ricky sucked his teeth, and then threw his cellphone on the couch; he addressed Bullet, as he sat down on the couch. "You hear from Shooter or hear anything about him?" Bullet looked at him and then shook his head. "Nope…I called around and nobody seen or heard from him." Ricky sat back against the couch, and then rubbed his hands down his face. "Fuck…" Another associate of Ricky's spoke. "I can ask around the streets; maybe he not in town no more." Ricky looked at the guy, and then shook his head. "Nah, don't worry about it…what about Jaquelyn?" Bullet made a sarcastic sound. "Which one?" Ricky rolled his eyes. "You know which one…the one walking around gettin' on everybody's fuckin' nerves." Bullet sighed and then made a drink at the bar; he shook his head. "Probably in Dallas with that nigga, Preston." Ricky sucked his teeth. Nothing was going as they all expected, and Maxwell wasn't the only one that couldn't take any more of this; everyone was fed up with how Jaquelyn was using Jovanni's body for evil and how reckless she was being.

Ricky lit a blunt and then the doorbell rang; another guy walked out the living room and then shortly after, he returned with Randall. The guy went to sit down and then Randall shook his head, as he went to sit down on the couch, next to Ricky. "Something happened…" Ricky turned his head to Randall. "What?" Randall sighed. "I got a call today…there was some fight or incident at the jail yesterday. I wasn't given all the details, but it was on lockdown and a couple of people got injured…including Jaquelyn or JoJo…whatever." Ricky frowned. "Is she alright?" Randall shrugged his shoulders. "She was unconscious when they found her…so they took her to the infirmary…I don't know anything else." Ricky sighed and then shook his head. "Fuck…JoJo been took off from here, and she ain't answering her damn phone. She might be in Dallas with that nigga Preston."

Randall nodded and then sighed. "Well, my attempts to block Jaquelyn's transfer, failed…she's supposed to be moved in a few days, but since this incident at the jail, I know that's on hold." Ricky nodded. "Yeah, alright…I'ma call Max and let him know what's going on." Randall nodded and then Ricky grabbed his cellphone from the couch; he dialed Maxwell's number and then put the phone to his ear.

Randall grabbed the blunt from Ricky, and then started to smoke it, as Bullet and others sat around.

Maxwell answered and Ricky sighed. "Hey, something happened at the jail yesterday…a lockdown 'cause of a fight or something. Jaquelyn was unconscious 'cause of the fight. I don't know all the details, but I'm just letting you know." Ricky listened and then frowned; he looked at Randall, who looked right back at him. "You sure that was yesterday? You seen her since?" Ricky listened and then put his hand over his face; he dropped it and then nodded. "Yeah…I got it; let me know if you hear something." Ricky ended the call and Randall frowned. "What?" Ricky shook his head. "Max said JoJo went to see Jaquelyn in jail yesterday…she was supposed to call him after she left, so they could talk, but she never did." Randall looked at Ricky and he frowned. "You think she had something to do with this and tried to attack Jaquelyn in jail? You think she figured it out?" Ricky shrugged his shoulders. "I don't know…Max said he went to see Jaquelyn in jail, and she told him to get JoJo there, so they could talk. Something must of went wrong…" Randall sighed, and then shook his head. "I don't know what to tell you…if I hear anything else, then I'll get back to you." Ricky nodded and then Randall passed the blunt back to him; afterwards, Randall stood from the couch and then told Ricky, goodbye. Ricky nodded and then Randall walked out the living room.

Ricky sighed and then looked at Bullet. "Keep trying to find Shooter…I need him back." Bullet nodded, and then he and another guy stood from the couch, to leave the living room. Ricky rubbed his hand down his face and then sighed.

# Chapter 22

Maxwell waited outside the door and then looked around; the door opened, and Maxwell turned his head. He did a doubletake and frowned. "Uh, is Mike here?" Kevin nodded. "Mr. Marshall, right? Mike's twin brother?" Maxwell slowly nodded his head, and Kevin stepped aside. Maxwell walked in the house, and then Kevin escorted him to the living room.

Once in the living room, Kevin spoke. "Mr. Marshall, your brother is here. I'ma go check on the boys and let me know when you want me to run your bath for you." Maxwell frowned, as Michael nodded. Kevin walked out the living room, and Maxwell looked at his brother. "Who is that?" Michael slightly laughed. "Kevin…my new nanny." Maxwell continued to frown and temporarily forgot why he was there. "Your new nanny? Really, Mike? Why is he shirtless?" Michael rolled his eyes, and then told his brother to sit down.

Maxwell shook his head, and then sat down next to his brother. "Where's Stacee?" Michael sighed. "Asleep…he's been working a new night job, but he's about to stop. I hired Kevin to work at night, while Stacee is gone." Maxwell made a sarcastic sound. "So, you have a guy walking around like that at night…in the house, when Stacee is gone?" Michael rolled his eyes. "I swear you sound just like Stacee…I'm not doing anything with Kevin." Maxwell nodded his head. "That's what you said about Stacee, but yet he's your man now, and still living with you. I don't even wanna know what words Stacee said to you, when he found out about this." Michael frowned. "Did you come over here to be dad? Because you're damn sure talking and acting like him." Maxwell gave his brother a snide look. "When the hell did we switch places? You used to get on my ass about how I was a dictator to my staff and help, and now that I stopped being like that, you decided to do it. I see you can't make your own drinks anymore either." Michael sucked his teeth. "Once again, why are you here, Max?" Maxwell sighed and then nodded. "Fine…your social life distracted me for a moment, but I'm back on track now. I wanted to let you know that Ricky called me. There was a lockdown at the jail yesterday, and Jaquelyn got hurt; she was unconscious and I'm assuming she was taken to the hospital, or however that works. I told him that JoJo went to see Jaquelyn in jail yesterday. I tried to call her after Ricky called me, but she's not answering. I don't know what's going on or what happened, but Jaquelyn's body is not in the best condition." Michael sighed and then shook his head. "Well, maybe JoJo had nothing to do with this. You said she kept getting in a fight with some dike at the jail, so maybe that's what happened, and JoJo wasn't able to get in the jail to see Jaquelyn." Maxwell sighed and then nodded. "It's possible…I was trying to hurry up and get her pregnant, before Preston knocked her up." Michael frowned. "Do what?" Maxwell sighed and then shook his head. "The last time I went to see JoJo, I told her what was going on with the real Jaquelyn and her body. About her wanting to get pregnant and having a baby, so JoJo told me to…she told me just to fuck her and get her pregnant, so when they switched back, she'd be pregnant with my baby and not Preston's."

Michael frowned the entire time that Maxwell spoke. "What the hell? This shit is getting more confusing and complicated by the day." Maxwell slightly nodded his head, and then rubbed his hands down his face. "Yeah, I know…a part of me wants Jaquelyn's body to die, but then that means that JoJo could die too. I'm so conflicted on how to feel about all this. Jax and Madison haven't seen their mama in months…they're growing up so fast; she's missing the most important parts. They're already holding their own bottles, and Madison is trying to crawl. JoJo is missing all of that."

Maxwell slightly looked down and Michael put his hand on his shoulder. "Max, just hold on…I'm sure just a little while longer and this'll all be over." Maxwell slightly nodded his head. "Yeah…" Michael nodded and then they both heard yelling and sounds of something hitting the walls. Michael frowned. "What the fuck?" Both men jumped up from the couch, and then ran towards where the sounds were coming from. It was coming from upstairs, so Michael and Maxwell ran up the stairs.

When the guys reached the top, they saw Kevin with his arm to Stacee's throat, and that he had Stacee pinned against the banister. The men ran over, and Michael grabbed Kevin to pull him back, while Maxwell grabbed Stacee before he fell over the banister. Stacee coughed hysterically, as Michael pushed Kevin back and then looked at him. "What the fuck is wrong with you?!" Kevin shook his head, as he breathed hard. "He started it…he punched me first, when I was trying to change Mikey." Stacee looked at him. "I told you I had it!" Michael looked at Stacee and frowned, as Maxwell continued to hold Stacee back. "He's the fucking nanny, Stacee! You were supposed to be asleep!" Stacee shot back. "I woke up!" Kevin sucked his teeth, and then looked at his hand. Maxwell sighed and then shook his head. "Uh, Mike…I need to go, so I'll talk to you later." Michael frowned. "Really? You're leaving now?" Maxwell let Stacee go and then walked over to his brother; he grinned, as he looked at him. "Good luck, Mr. Marshall…" Maxwell slightly laughed on the way down the stairs. Michael sighed and then rubbed his hands down his face; he looked at Stacee. "Go to bed…" He looked at Kevin. "Clean yourself up…" Michael shook his head, as he walked away. "I'll change the boys…" Both guys watched Michael walk in the nursery, and then they looked at each other. Kevin rolled his eyes, and then turned around to walk to his bedroom. Stacee sucked his teeth, and then walked to the nursery.

Stacee walked in and then saw Michael changing Mikey on the changing table. He walked over to Michael, and then put his arms around him. "I'm sorry…" Michael slightly nodded his head. "What happened to the deal?" Stacee stepped back from Michael and then sighed. "It's a habit…I heard one of the boys crying and I got up; that's what I'm used to doing." Michael finished changing Mikey and then picked him up; he turned around to Stacee. "Is it also a habit to punch the help? I've never assaulted my help before, and I'm hoping I don't get sued over this now." Stacee sighed and then nodded. "I'm sorry…I'll let that bitch do his job." Michael frowned. "I'll pretend I didn't hear that…I'll go apologize to him." Stacee raised an eyebrow. "No, you won't…but you can tell him to start putting on clothes when he's working. This is still a job, not his damn house; he don't need to be comfortable here."

Michael rolled his eyes and then nodded. "Are you done? I swear you're fucking cranky when you wake up…" Stacee sighed. "Tell me the truth, Mike…why him? Why'd you hire him? You could of got a little old lady that looks like a grandma to watch the twins." Michael sighed. "In case you forgot…I have twins. I need somebody that can move quick, handle stress, and has patience. I can't get that with an elderly man or woman, Stacee; that's why I hired him. He's athletic and can take those stairs three at a damn time, if he wanted; he has perfect hearing and can hear the boys from downstairs; he has twenty/twenty vision. He can also move around for an extended amount of time, without getting tired. That's why I hired him…it had nothing to do with how he looks. I know what he was doing before, and those same qualities that women wanted him for, works for my situation, except I don't want sex from him."

Stacee slightly nodded his head. "The same reasons you kept me as your nanny, right?" Michael slightly nodded his head. "Yeah..." Stacee sighed and then nodded. "Ok...I'll leave him alone and let him do his job. I won't say anything else about this again." Stacee said nothing else, as he turned around and then walked out the nursery. Michael sighed and then looked at Mikey, who had his fingers in his mouth. "Are you hungry?" Mikey looked at him and he slightly smiled. "Don't worry, Mikey...Stacee's not going anywhere, no matter how much I wanna choke him sometimes." Michael shook his head and then walked to the mini fridge in the nursery; he took a bottle out and then sat down with Mikey. He handed Mikey the bottle and then held him in the chair, while Mickey was asleep.

# Chapter 23

It was the next day, and Nathan was in Dallas; he rang the doorbell and then shortly after, Cyrus opened the door. He smiled when he saw his brother. "Hey, I didn't know you were coming in town." Nathan slightly nodded his head. "Uh, yeah…I was gonna call first, but…" Cyrus frowned, as he stepped aside, so his brother could come in. "Nate, what's wrong?" Nathan cleared his throat, as Cyrus closed the door. He looked at his brother. "Nate…" Nathan looked at Cyrus and then sighed. "Come have a drink with me." Cyrus slightly nodded his head. "Alright…" Both men walked to the living room, and then Cyrus went to the kitchen to get him and his brother a beer. Nathan sat down on the couch and then rubbed his hands down his face, as he waited.

Cyrus returned to the living room and then sat down on the couch. "Nothing hard around here lately, just beer." Nathan took the beer and then nodded. "It's fine, Cyrus…" Cyrus popped the top off his beer and then took a sip, as he looked at his brother. "Nate, what's wrong? You and Bella got something going on?" Nathan stared straight. "Uh, Randall called me this morning. Apparently, a couple of days ago there was an incident at the jail; Jaquelyn was injured and moved from the infirmary to the hospital." Cyrus slightly frowned. "Is she alright?" Nathan set the beer on the coffee table, and then looked back at Cyrus. "No, Cyrus…she's not alright; she's gone…she died this morning." Cyrus stared at his brother and then shook his head. "Jaquelyn is dead? Wait a minute, Nate…what about JoJo?" Cyrus abruptly stood from the couch and dropped the beer bottle at the same time. "JoJo was in Jaquelyn's body…so what happened to JoJo? She didn't switch back yet; she hadn't switched back yet…so JoJo's dead?"

Nathan sniffed, and then stood from the couch; he looked at his brother. "Yeah, Cyrus…I'm sorry…I'm so sorry." Cyrus stepped back from his brother and then slowly shook his head. "No, Nate…no, not my baby girl!" Nathan quickly grabbed Cyrus and tried to restrain him, because he was hysterical. "Let me go! Not my baby girl!" Cyrus cried hard, and then went down to the floor, with Nathan still holding him. He continued to cry hard, as Bernadine hurried into the living room, as fast as she could; she had never heard those sounds before and definitely not from Cyrus.

Bernadine entered the living room and then stopped. "Cyrus…what's wrong?" She looked at Nathan. "Nate, what's going on?" Nathan turned his head to Bernadine with red and watery eyes. "Jaquelyn's body is dead…she died this morning." Bernadine put her hand on her stomach, and then slightly shook her head. "Her body is dead, so that means…JoJo." Nathan nodded and Bernadine put her hand to her mouth; she cried and then slowly sat down on the armchair.

Cyrus continued to wail, while deeply in pain; his heart hurt from the loss of his daughter. Bernadine started to breathe hard, as she cried. She put her hand to her stomach again and then winced in pain. Nathan turned his head to her. "Cyrus…Cyrus…it's Dina." Cyrus looked at Bernadine, and then shook his head, as he continued to cry. "Baby…what's wrong? Baby…" Cyrus got up from the floor, and then hurried over to her, as she yelled out. Nathan got up from the floor and then ran over too. "Cyrus!" Cyrus and Nathan helped her up from the chair and she continued to yell. Bernadine was seven months pregnant and was in labor; the abrupt stress had skyrocketed her blood pressure, after hearing about Jaquelyn's death and seeing Cyrus's reaction.

Both men grabbed Bernadine and then Nathan told Cyrus they were taking her to the hospital, instead of calling for an ambulance; he had to get himself together, which was hard, since he was still impacted with the thought of never hearing Jovanni's voice again. Both men hurried to take Bernadine out the house and then to the car, so they could leave.

# Chapter 24

Michael hurried over to his brother's house and didn't bother ringing the doorbell; he banged on the door several times until it opened. Michael was breathing hard. "Where is he?" Angeline was crying when she opened the door. "In his office…" Michael nodded, and then she moved out the way. Michael ran in the house and then to his brother's office; he heard him on the other side of the door. Michael flung the door open and then found his brother on the floor with a bottle of vodka, while crying hard. Michael shook his head, as he slowly walked over to his brother. "Max, I'm sorry…" Maxwell shook his head, as Michael looked around the destroyed office. There were books everywhere and everything that was on the desk, was now on the floor. The desk was damaged, and the curtains were pulled halfway down.

After Maxwell received the call about Jaquelyn, he immediately reacted, as they all did. Jaquelyn's body was gone and that meant that Jovanni's personality was gone as well.

Michael went over to his brother, and then knelt down to him. "Max..." Maxwell looked at his brother, as he continued to cry. "Why? Why?" Michael shook his head. "I don't know, Max..." Maxwell took another gulp from the bottle and some of the alcohol fell from his mouth; he let it fall and then slightly shook his head. "Nothing matters anymore...I have to raise Jax and Madison without their mama now. Jaquelyn did something to her; I know she did...JoJo must of told her when she went to see her in jail. Jaquelyn killed JoJo's personality to keep her quiet...so she'd never get out. So, she could keep being JoJo!"

Maxwell put his hand over his face, and then cried hard, as Michael sighed. "Max, I know..." Michael's cellphone rang, before he could finish his sentence; he quickly took his cellphone from his pocket and answered. "Hello..." Michael frowned and then looked at Maxwell. "What? Now? We're on our way..." Michael ended the call, and then shook his head, as Maxwell looked at him. "What now?" Michael sighed. "That was Nathan...mama is in the hospital; she went into labor early and she's in bad shape." Maxwell frowned. "What? No...I can't, please I can't do this...not now..." Michael nodded and then helped his brother up from the floor. "Come on, Max, I got you...I got you; we have to go." Maxwell nodded, as his brother helped him up. Maxwell dropped the bottle on the floor. Then they left the office, and Michael drove them both to the hospital.

*   *   *

Cyrus was at the hospital, along with Nathan and Bella; he called her on the way to the hospital. Bernadine was rushed away, as soon as they entered the hospital. Cyrus was seated and silently crying to himself, while bouncing his leg up and down. Nathan was standing, while Bella was seated in a chair. Malcolm almost crashed his car into Michael's car in the parking lot. Michael called their dad on the way to the hospital. The three men hurried to the floor where Bernadine had been taken.

Once there, Nathan turned his head and saw the condition that Maxwell was in and knew he was still feeling as Cyrus was, in regards to the news of Jaquelyn's death.

Michael went over to Cyrus and saw that he was distraught, so looked at Nathan. "What did they say?" Nathan shook his head. "We don't know anything yet..." Michael nodded and then went back over to Maxwell; he told him to sit down, and he nodded.

Maxwell slowly sat down and then started to cry a little. Malcolm looked at his son and was told by Michael on the phone, about Jaquelyn. Malcolm went over to Maxwell and then sat down next to him; he put his arm around him, as Bella sighed. Nathan rubbed his hands down his face and then the doctor came out. Everyone either looked up or turned their heads. Cyrus shot up from the chair, and then went over to the doctor. "My wife...how's my wife? How's the baby?" The doctor slightly nodded his head. "We had to do an emergency c-section on your wife; your daughter is two months early and only three pounds, but she's just fine and will be fine in our NICU." Cyrus slightly nodded. "My daughter…?" The doctor nodded and then continued. "Your wife…she's not doing so good; she hemorrhaged and lost an extensive amount of blood, before we did the emergency c-section. Her blood pressure went up extremely high and then she started to have a seizure after we took the baby. She's on a ventilator now…and I have to be honest with you, Mr. Mann…it doesn't look good, so maybe you and your family should start making arrangements now to say goodbye."

Cyrus felt as if he was about to have a heart attack. "Goodbye?" Bella put her hand to her mouth and silently cried, as Nathan slightly looked down. Michael and Maxwell looked at each other, and then back to the doctor. Cyrus lost it. "Goodbye?! I'm not saying goodbye to my damn wife! I didn't get a chance to say goodbye to my damn daughter!" Cyrus fell to the floor. "I can't take this! I can't take this, please!" Nathan went over to his brother, as Bella cried hard with her hand to her mouth. Maxwell sat back down and then put both hands over his face, as he cried. Michael stayed standing and sniffed, as he cried. Malcolm rubbed his hands down his face and then sniffed, as tears fell from his eyes. Cyrus wasn't the only one that couldn't take this: Maxwell couldn't either. Cyrus didn't think he would make it through this and felt he didn't have the strength to endure this much hurt and pain at once.

# Chapter 25

It was the end of the week and Jaquelyn's funeral; everyone was there, and she was buried in Dallas. They were all outside and sitting in chairs, in front of the casket that was to be lowered after the speeches. Cyrus stared at that casket and couldn't look anywhere else; Bella was on one side of him, and Nathan was on the other. Maxwell sat in the front row with them, with Michael beside him. Stacee was there and had the boys, while Angeline had the twins; Allen, Clemmons, and Mr. Henry were there. Malcolm was there with Ashanti and Kennedy. Ricky, Randall, and Bullet were there; Trey, Deon, Auston, Aubrey, Desiray, Mariya, and Kentay were seated. Lydia was sitting in the back.

The funeral director stood at the podium behind the casket and then began. "Jaquelyn Harris was a beautiful woman, inside and out…" Maxwell rolled his eyes, as some sighed. Ricky slightly shook his head, as he stared at the funeral director, who continued. "She was a spirited woman who…" Maxwell interjected. "Stop…" The funeral director stopped, and everyone looked at Maxwell; he stood from his chair, and then walked to the podium. Maxwell looked at the funeral director and told him to move; the man cleared his throat and then nodded. He moved out the way and then sat down, as Maxwell stood at the podium with red eyes, and looked around at everyone. "That gravestone says Jaquelyn Harris…the damn paper in everybody's hand says Jaquelyn Harris, but I think it's irrelevant now to keep the damn charade going, because we all know why we're here. JoJo was killed in that damn jail, not Jaquelyn. We're here for JoJo…and her only." Michael sighed, as Cyrus stared at him with tears streaming down his cheeks.

Maxwell shook his head, as he became emotional. "Jaquelyn Harris's body is dead…and along with her body, died Jovanni Mann's personality. I'm here for JoJo…like I know everybody else is. I lost my soulmate…my kids lost their mama; I lost the other half of my heart…" Desiray's lips quivered, as she listened to Maxwell. Trey sniffed, as he slightly looked down. Everyone was emotional and crying. Ricky tried his hardest to hold his tears in but failed; he kept the same blank expression on his face, as the tears left his eyes.

Maxwell continued. "I am sorry to Cyrus, Ricky, and Lydia for the loss of their daughter…but I won't downplay how much pain I'm in right now, knowing that I'll never hear JoJo's voice again. I'll never see JoJo again, because I refuse to accept the woman that's walking around free somewhere, in my woman's body…and we all know who the hell that is; and if you don't know, then you might as well get up from your chair and walk away, because we're not here for Jaquelyn." Lydia sighed and then swallowed hard, as Cyrus cried harder than he was before, but silently.

Maxwell wiped his eyes, and then took a deep breath. "I won't ever understand why things happen…I still can't understand right now, what already transpired in the first place. But I can only hope that everybody here will find some peace from this tragedy and not question anymore of why this happened, because I've been doing it, since I received the news and it's done nothing but make me sick every day, since. My children' will know how much I loved their mama and know how much she loved them. Her memory will never die, and I know I won't be the only one to keep JoJo's memory alive. She's in all of us…in me and in my children, when I look at them." Maxwell looked down at the casket, and then his lips quivered. "I love you, baby…" Maxwell walked away from the podium and then went to sit back down; he looked down and then put his hands over his face, as he cried hard and loudly. This somewhat gave everyone the greenlight to do the same; hearing Maxwell break down the way he did, made everyone lose it. The crying started and continued, as everyone was trying to comfort each other.

The gravediggers moved the arrangements out the way and then the lowering of Jaquelyn's casket began. Cyrus shook his head. "No…no, wait!" Cyrus tried to stop the casket, and Nathan quickly grabbed his brother, since he almost fell in the grave. "No, wait! JoJo!" Nathan held his brother back, as Ashanti put her hand over her face and cried. Desiray and Mariya were crying hard, as well. Randall shook his head, as Ricky sniffed and then wiped his eyes.

After the casket was lowered, everyone stood from the chairs; many had to be helped up. Trey helped Mariya up, as Deon grabbed Desiray, when it seemed she was about to pass out. After a short walk away from the gravesite, everyone got in their vehicles to leave, or in Maxwell's case, in the limo. They all went back to Maxwell's house.

# Chapter 26

One month later…

Cyrus was packing when the doorbell rang; he stopped what he was doing, and then walked to the front. When he reached the door, he opened it and then nodded to Maxwell and Michael. He stepped aside, and then they walked in. Cyrus closed the door and then returned to the living room, as they followed him.

Once back in the living room, Cyrus returned to what he was doing. Michael and Maxwell stood there, as he spoke. "What can I do for you boys?" Michael looked at Maxwell, and then back to Cyrus. "Uh, you missed mama's will reading today, so we came to check on you." Cyrus slightly nodded his head, as he taped the box up. "Yeah, I know…I didn't need to be there." Michael sighed. "Actually, you did need to be there…you were mama's husband."

Cyrus stopped what he was doing and then sighed; he sat down on top of the box and then finally looked up at the boys. "These past few weeks been too much for me…I lost my daughter and my wife; now I have to raise your baby sister alone. The last thing on my mind is a will reading that I don't got nothing to do with." Maxwell slightly nodded his head. "Well, where are you going?" Cyrus sighed and then grabbed his cigarettes off another box; he lit one and then got back to the boys. "This is Dina's house…so I'm moving back to Houston, after Deana is released from the hospital. I'ma stay with Nate until I can get back on my feet." Michael shook his head. "Cyrus, you should of went to the will reading, because…" Cyrus interjected. "Why? I'm only here because of my wife…" Cyrus swallowed hard, and then cleared his throat. "I'm sorry…" Michael nodded, and Maxwell sighed. "Cyrus…the house is yours, and mama left you the majority of her estate. You can stay…and live in your house now, with Deana."

Cyrus looked between them, and then slightly frowned, as he stood from the box. "I don't understand. Why'd she do that?" Maxwell raised an eyebrow, and then shook his head. "Cyrus, mama loved you…she married you; you made her happy from the time she met you. She had her will redone, the sixth month of her pregnancy. She added her grandchildren…me and Mike's twins; she added you and the baby that you two were going to have. She wanted you and Deana to be taken care of in case something happened to her. So, you can't leave…believe me, I know how you feel. I lost JoJo and my mama, so I'm still not doing too good, but you don't have to worry about whether or not you can take care of Deana and provide for her, because we're telling you now, that you can."

Maxwell walked over to Cyrus and then handed him the big manila envelope. Cyrus took the envelope and then sighed, as Maxwell slightly stepped back. "Everything you need is in that envelope…the deed to the house, spare keys, bank account numbers, passwords…it's all there. And if you have any questions about anything, our family attorney's card is in there too."

Cyrus sniffed, as he looked up at Maxwell with red eyes. "How can I stay here? She gave her life for a baby she wanted so much. Why did she stay pregnant? We could of been happy right now, together…" Michael walked over to them, and then stopped. "Cyrus, she loved you that much that she wanted a part of you; she just loved you that much…" Cyrus nodded and then stood from the box; he put the cigarette out and then rubbed his hand down his face. Cyrus took a deep breath and then sniffed again, as he nodded. "Ok…I'll stay, but uh…I don't know how, I mean when Deana gets out the hospital, I need to work and…" Michael interjected. "We'll take care of that…we'll make sure Deana has a nanny to take care of her when you work, but right now and maybe for a month after Deana gets out the hospital, it's ok for you to take time off from work. I know you're not used to this, but you have money now, Cyrus. There's no more struggling on this end, regardless, because we're all here for you and Deana. And we'll keep being here…so if you need anything then you give us a call, even dad."

Cyrus looked between the boys and then nodded; he reached forward and then hugged Maxwell, as he thanked him. Cyrus hugged Michael and then afterwards, he nodded. Maxwell said they were leaving. Cyrus told them goodbye and then watched them both walk out the living room. Afterwards, Cyrus sat down on the couch with the manila envelope, and then looked at it; he then started to cry again, as he shook his head.

* * *

Michael was driving back to the office, with Maxwell in the passenger seat. Michael glanced at Maxwell and then sighed. "Can you believe we're all single fathers now?" Maxwell looked at his brother and then back straight. "Actually, I can…Cyrus hadn't gotten over this anymore than we have. Do you really believe that mama gave her life for Deana?" Michael sighed, and then nodded his head. "I do…you know how mama was and how damn happy she was. I don't think I've ever been as happy as she was in the end. She wanted this baby, and I think a part of her knew that she might not survive that pregnancy. Cyrus meant everything to her, and I think she's still happy knowing that she gave him a child before she passed."

Maxwell took a deep breath and then sniffed. "I can't handle any more death or despair…any more bad news. I'm trying to move on, and I'm still getting flowers and cards sent to the damn house over Jaquelyn's death. We've been divorced for two damn years, and I'm getting condolences over her. Every time I get something, I think about JoJo and how everybody must not of known how much I loved her, to think that

138

I'd be grieving over Jaquelyn that hard, when I didn't even love her." Michael shook his head and then looked at his brother, before looking back at the road. "Don't do that, Max…those who mattered, knew how much you loved JoJo. Everybody else are strangers that didn't know a damn thing about your life or Jaquelyn's to think any different." Maxwell nodded. "Yeah well, this moving forward is not gonna happen for me. I don't want another woman, and I'm not going out looking for a mother for my children. I'd rather have them grow up motherless, like JoJo did, than replace her…"

Michael looked at his brother, and then back to the road; he sighed. "I understand…I guess I'm doing the same." Maxwell looked at his brother and then slightly laughed, as he shook his head. "I think my situation is different than yours, Mike…you have a second daddy for your boys, and he already lives there." Michael rolled his eyes, and then shook his head. "Stacee is not my boys' daddy…" Maxwell raised an eyebrow. "He might as well be, since he's raising the boys with you. He's been there for them since they were a few months old, Mike, and he's still there…that's a damn daddy." Michael looked at Maxwell, and then back to the road; he said nothing, as he thought about what his brother said.

Shortly after, they reached the law firm and then Michael parked in his spot; they both got out the car and then buttoned their suit jackets, as they walked to the entrance. They only had a few more hours of work and then they were done for the day.

# Chapter 27

After a few more hours at work, Michael returned home and then hung his keys on the wall; he did his usual routine of going to his office first before going to the living room. Once in the living room, he slightly frowned. "Hey, I thought you were at work." Stacee put his hands in his pockets and then nodded. "I was, but I got off early. I told Kevin he could go, if that's alright." Michael nodded, as he loosened his tie. "Yeah, that's fine…so why'd you get off early? Is something wrong?" Michael walked to the bar, as Stacee watched him. "I don't know, is there? I know you needed time to grieve after your mama died, and I gave you that. We been doing fly-bys with each other ever since. I just wanna know if you're good." Michael slightly nodded his head, as he took a sip of his drink; he then turned around at the bar. "I'm fine…never been better."

Michael walked away from the bar, and then over to the couch to sit down, as Stacee spoke. "Never been better? You watched your brother lose the love of his life…your mama died right after…" Michael interjected. "I know!" Stacee closed his mouth and then sighed, as he slightly nodded his head. "Alright, well I guess I'll keep leaving you alone." Stacee was about to turn around and walk away, when he heard Michael. "What do you want from me?" Stacee looked back at Michael. "What?" Michael shook his head, as he stared at Stacee. "What do you want from me? Do you want me to take care of you…are you trying to be a better daddy than me?" Stacee frowned. "What are you talking about, Mike?" Michael made a sarcastic sound, and then took another sip of his drink. "My brother did lose the love of his life…my mama gave her life, for the love of her life. You're here and been here for a while, so what do you want? Are you in this for the long haul or just long enough for the boys to get attached to you, before you walk out their lives too, like their mama did?"

Stacee continued to frown, as he listened to Michael and then shook his head. "Mike, I don't know where any of this is coming from, or what long haul you're talking about, but I'm not going nowhere…unless you tell me to. I'm trying to be with you…I been trying to be with you, but you act like you don't want that sometimes; like I'm in your way of something greater. You should be asking yourself what you want, instead of me, because you already know what I want."

Michael stared at Stacee, and then slowly nodded his head; he took another sip of his drink and then set it on the coffee table. Michael then rubbed his hands down his face, before looking back at Stacee. "I can't go through what my brother did…or Cyrus. I know there's no guarantees but something my brother said to me earlier, hit a nerve." Stacee walked over to Michael and then sat down next to him. "What he say?" Michael sighed. "He said you've been here for the boys since they were a few months old, and still here for them…that's a daddy." Stacee slightly nodded his head. "So that pissed you off or something? I can't replace you, Mike, and I'm not trying to…I'm just there for them like you are, like…" Michael interjected. "Like a daddy…" Stacee sighed, as he turned his head to the side. Michael slightly smiled. "I love you…and I want you here with me and the boys, but I need to know if you're in this with me for the long haul…because they're not the only ones that can get attached to you."

Stacee looked back at Michael and then smiled. "Yeah, I'm in this with you; I love you. I'm not going nowhere, but Kevin is…" Michael slightly laughed, as Stacee did too. Stacee slowed down his laughing and then smiled. "For real, it's time for Kevin to go…all the making drinks and running baths and shit, nobody else should be doing anything like that for you, but me. And I don't need you to take care of me, Mike…I wanna work, but I do see taking care of the boys as my job too. For them, I won't work…maybe for a while, if you want me to do that. But you gotta remember that it's us now and not just you. And yeah, Mikey and Mickey have two daddies, they always have…I'm just happy you finally realized that." Michael slightly nodded his head and then leaned in to kiss Stacee. Afterwards, he pulled back from him and smiled. "That's all I needed to know…" Stacee nodded and then stood from the couch; he sighed, as he looked at Michael. "You wanna go get the boys and bring them downstairs?" Michael nodded and then stood from the couch; he and Stacee then walked out the living room, to go get the boys.

# Chapter 28

Ricky was leaned against Bullet's car, while talking with him and a few guys; a car drove up to the house that Ricky or none of the guys recognized. Ricky eyed the car and then slightly squinted his eyes, as he stared at it. "Y'all know who that is?" The guys shook their heads no, and then Ricky slowly eased his hand in front of his shirt; he had his hand on his pistol, as the car stopped, and then the driver got out. Ricky raised an eyebrow and then Bullet frowned. "Is that a bitch or a nigga?" Ricky looked at him and then back to the driver, who walked up to the guys and then stopped; she looked between all of them. "I'm looking for Ricky Del Monte?" Ricky frowned, as he stared at the unidentified person in front of him. "Who the fuck is askin'…?" She looked at him. "I'm Timber, a jailhouse mate of Jaquelyn's…she told me to come to you when

I got out, and you'd have work for me."

Bullet looked at Ricky, while he was confused. "Jaquelyn told you that, when?" Timber sighed. "Before she died…I helped her out with some shit in jail and she said to come to you, so I'm here." Ricky looked around at the guys and then back to Timber. "Look, I don't know you like that, and Jaquelyn was never in jail, so I know you lyin'…" Timber slowly nodded her head. "My bad…I forgot; I mean, JoJo…" Ricky frowned and then stared at Timber for a few seconds, before speaking. "What you know about JoJo?" Timber slightly laughed. "Something about being in the wrong body…she came in Jaquelyn, but I don't know if she ever made it out." Bullet was confused. "Made it out of what?" Timber looked around and then back to Ricky. "Jaquelyn said she ain't know if it was gonna work or not, but she had to try. We started that shit at the jail the day of the lockdown; me and a guard had her back…JoJo came to see Jaquelyn and then the plan was in motion. The alarms went off and she had three minutes. Jaquelyn beat her sister's ass and then I was supposed to slam Jaquelyn's head against the wall to knock her out. Then me and the guard left, so they'd be found by other guards."

Ricky kept the frown on his face, as he listened to all of that. "Why y'all do that?" Timber sucked her teeth. "Jaquelyn said that happened before and she needed her and her sister to be unconscious at the same time, for them to switch back or something. I mean, I don't know what else went down. They had everybody locked down about time they found Jaquelyn and her sister in the room. But then I heard Jaquelyn died. I don't know what happened to her sister…she said her name was really JoJo and her sister was Jaquelyn in her body. That if it worked, then she'd get her body back, but since Jaquelyn died, I don't know if JoJo got her body back or not." Ricky looked at Bullet. "Call Randall…" Bullet nodded and then went in the house, as the other guys followed behind. Afterwards, Ricky looked around, and then told Timber to follow him in the house; she nodded.

Once back in the house, Ricky told Timber to have a seat, and she did. Ricky told one of his associates to get her a drink and he nodded. Ricky sat down on the couch and then lit a blunt, as Timber stared at him. He looked back at her. "The story is true…you were locked up with JoJo, not Jaquelyn. We had Jaquelyn's funeral…for her body, but mourned JoJo's personality, 'cause we ain't know shit about what went down in the jail. We thought Jaquelyn was there to kill JoJo's personality and end it, so Jaquelyn could stay out and take over JoJo's body." Timber shook her head. "It fucked me up to listen to that, but something in her damn eyes told me she wasn't making nothing up."

The guy walked over to Timber and then gave her the drink; she nodded to him and then Ricky sighed, as smoke came out his mouth. "The thing is, Timber…JoJo is missing. I didn't know she was in the same state that Jaquelyn was in the jail that day. Wasn't no calls or nothing from nobody and she ain't answer her phone since, so…" Timber interjected. "I got her stuff…JoJo told me to take it off the body, so she couldn't be identified when they took her to the hospital." Ricky frowned, as Timber reached in the pockets of her baggy jeans, and then pulled out the cellphone, wallet, and ID. She handed the items to

Ricky; he took them and then looked at them. Ricky then looked back at Timber. "This shit for real?" Timber nodded. "Yeah…JoJo said if this didn't work and her personality died, then to kill her body…Jaquelyn, if she didn't die too." Ricky slowly nodded his head. "I'd do that, if I knew where the fuck she was. It's been over a damn month and no word, so…" Ricky frowned, as Bullet took the phone from his ear; he heard the conversation and then looked at Ricky, as the look was returned.

Bullet slightly nodded his head. "Jaquelyn ain't got survival skills, Ricky…so she either dead, or it worked." Ricky put his hand up to him. "Nah, Jaquelyn was ghost after she stabbed JoJo." Bullet interjected. "But she stayed with that dude, Preston…she wasn't on her own. She left him and then went to Bellfort Randy, then we got her." Ricky sighed and then shook his head. "Go to the office and look up any hospital admission shit for the day of the lockdown; they took JoJo's body somewhere, so the closest hospital to the jail in Dallas." Bullet nodded and then stood from the couch; he walked out the living room and then Ricky looked back at Timber. "What JoJo say about what I do?" Timber made a sarcastic sound. "That it ain't legit, but it's work, and I'd make money…she said y'all would take care of me when I got out, if I helped her." Ricky slightly nodded his head. "Yeah, that sounds like JoJo…look here, we gonna get this shit situated and then I'ma find something for you to do." Timber nodded and then Ricky continued. "You know anything else…where JoJo would go if this worked?" Timber shook her head no and Ricky nodded. "Alright…"

Bullet returned to the living room and then grinned when he looked at Ricky. "Unidentified female taken to the hospital from the jail that day…in a coma for three days from an allergic reaction to an anesthesia…" Timber interjected. "Yeah, that's her…JoJo said she was allergic to that shit, and it'd do her damage; the guard gave her a syringe of that shit to inject in her sister. That's why I had to slam Jaquelyn's head against the wall to knock her out, 'cause she wasn't allergic to nothing." Ricky frowned and then looked back at Bullet. "So, it's her? What happened to her?" Bullet sighed. "She came out her coma and then left the hospital…" Ricky put his blunt out in the ashtray, and then rubbed his hands down his face; he then slowly nodded his head. "She's alive…but which one of them is alive?" Bullet shook his head. "We find her, then we get our answer…" Ricky nodded. "Yeah, alright…and if we do find her and she's not JoJo…then I'ma put a bullet in that bitch myself."


To be continued…

# Epilogue

One month before…

Shooter was in the kitchen of an apartment, when he heard a knock at the door; he turned his head and then slightly frowned. Shooter walked out the kitchen and then to the front door; he looked through the peephole and then slightly stepped back. Shooter sighed and then opened the door; he then abruptly had a gun aimed at him. Shooter put his hands up and then backed away from the door, as Jovanni walked in; she then closed the door behind her and locked it. Shooter sighed and then dropped his hands. "So, you gonna shoot me now? You already got me kicked out Ricky's house, so what else you want?" Jovanni shook her head, as she kept the gun aimed at him; he saw the condition she was in and then slightly frowned. "Where you been, a UFC match?"

Jovanni didn't appreciate his sarcasm. "I need money..." Shooter made a sarcastic sound and then turned around to walk back to the kitchen. Jovanni frowned. "Come back!" Shooter waved his hand around. "Fuck you, JoJo...if you gonna shoot me, then do it." Jovanni lowered her arm with the gun and then walked to the kitchen.

Shooter went back to cutting the cocaine on the counter. Jovanni frowned, after she walked in the kitchen. "That's what you're doing now?" Shooter glanced at her and then went back to what he was doing. "This what I been doing...for years. I just gotta do it by myself now, to live. Why the fuck you care? Leave me alone...I won't tell nobody you was here." Jovanni slightly nodded her head. "I need money...please." Shooter sighed and then looked at her. "Do I look like I got money to spare, JoJo? You fucked up my life! You got me kicked out the only fuckin' home I ever knew! Now you askin' me for money?!" Jovanni sighed, as Shooter clenched his jaw. "You might got that gun in your hand...but trust me, when I say that I'm still more dangerous than you, and I bet I can snap you in half, before you pull the fuckin' trigger." Jovanni slightly nodded her head. "Why don't you do it?" Shooter slightly shrugged his shoulders. "I can't...I just can't...I can't touch you." Jovanni slightly nodded her head, and then put the gun back behind her. "If you can't give me money, then I need a place to stay instead." Shooter had turned his head back to what he was doing and when he heard that, he stopped. He slowly turned his head back to Jovanni. "You gotta be fuckin' kidding me. You not stayin' here and you not gettin' no damn money from me either. Get the fuck out and go back to doing whatever the fuck you was doing." Jovanni slightly nodded her head. "If I apologize for what I did to you, will you let me stay?" Shooter had enough and then walked over to Jovanni; he was in her face. "No…what the fuck don't you understand about the word, no?" Jovanni sighed and then slightly nodded her head; she then leaned in and whispered something in Shooter's ear. Shooter listened and then frowned; she pulled back from him, and he looked at her, as she spoke. "Where do I sleep?" Shooter stared at her for a few moments and then swallowed hard. "Down the hall…to the right." Jovanni nodded and then turned around to walk out the kitchen, as he watched her. Afterwards, he cleared his throat, and then went back to the counter to finish what he was doing; he turned his head out the kitchen, and then slightly shook his head.

# JAKLEENA 'J' WARE

Is an Independent author who currently lives in Spring, Texas, and has five children. She is a 2001 graduate of El Campo High School in El Campo, Texas. She received two associates degrees, in Occupational Studies for Auto Cad/Drafting and another in Applied Sciences for Paralegal. Her first series entitled, **Family Affairs**, has thirty-one volumes; her second series entitled, **The Toll Road Girls**, has twelve parts; her third series entitled, **Justified**, has twenty-eight volumes; and her fourth series entitled, **Fontaine**, has thirty parts. Her fifth series entitled, **Sidelines**, has seventeen parts. All series are available on Amazon and Kindle. This is her sixth series entitled, **TwinInsanity**, and this is part seven.